'LEAD THOU ME ON'

'LEAD THOU ME ON'

REFLECTIONS FROM LAKE PAPAKEECHIE

REV. VINCENT J. GIESE

Our Sunday Visitor Publishing Division
Our Sunday Visitor, Inc.
Huntington, Indiana 46750

Our Sunday Visitor Publishing Division
Our Sunday Visitor, Inc.
200 Noll Plaza
Huntington, Indiana 46750

International Standard Book Number: 0-87973-533-3
Library of Congress Catalog Card Number 93-83257

PRINTED IN THE UNITED STATES OF AMERICA

Cover design by Rebecca J. Heaston

533

For Tony.

Affectionately yours,

"Geese"

CONTENTS

(continued)

CONTENTS
(continued)

PREFACE:

On the Banks of Lake Papakeechie

AT the lakes of Wawasee and Papakeechie in Northern Indiana, legend has it that Chief Papakeechie, the most influential of the Miami chiefs, and his brother, Chief Wawasee, fought in the battle of Tippecanoe.

At the time of the arrival of the white man, Chief Papakeechie was about sixty years old, corpulent, and prosaically known as "Flat Belly." In 1828, his reservation, ceded to him by the government and returned to the government in 1834, was about six miles square, with a town of seventy-five inhabitants.

Be that as it may, in 1900 the lakes of Wawasee and Papakeechie were developed side by side: Wawasee, the largest natural lake in Indiana, and Papakeechie, a tiny fishing lake. In size and contrast, the two lakes couldn't be more different. Lake Papakeechie, where no motors are allowed, banked by spacious lots and a wilderness, is a fisherman's paradise, whereas Lake Wawasee is a large boating lake with spacious homes and cottages, water skiing and swimming.

I made my home-away-from-home at Lake Papakeechie from 1980 until 1990, located somewhere between Fort Wayne and South Bend, Indiana. I often refer to it as Lake Galilee.

It was September 1988, overlooking the beautiful sunset of Lake Papakeechie, that I cried.

I had just returned from Zambia, in central Africa, when I realized this was my last trip to the Third World nations. I had just finished my ten years at Our Sunday Visitor, a publisher, just forty miles from Lake Papakeechie. It was time to chart a new course.

As I cried, part of my tears were of joy that I was returning to Chicago, where I had become a priest some twenty-three years ago to serve the Archdiocese of Chicago; but most of my tears were of sadness to leave the Fort Wayne-South Bend Diocese, the place of my birth, and particularly Lake Papakeechie, which had become such a vital part of my life as a priest-journalist.

Lake Papakeechie had been good to me the past ten years. It gave me the inner peace and a holy space, a place to entertain friends, to regroup my inner forces after many gruelling trips to the Third World nations.

Chicago seemed far away from Lake Papakeechie, just as Jerusalem was far away from Lake Galilee. I have always had a love-hate relationship with Chicago. As Jesus cried over Jerusalem, I too cried over Chicago. I felt, in September 1988, that I would soon lose my little cottage, and it brought tears to my overflowing heart. Within a year, I would give up the cottage at Lake Papakeechie.

Something in me died with that separation. In a sense, the small cottage had embodied my work the past ten years, as a priest and as a journalist. It meant a separation from my relatives, my classmates at Central Catholic High School in Fort Wayne (we celebrated our fiftieth reunion the summer of 1991). It meant a separation from pastoral ministry at St. John's parish; St. Mary's, the inner-city parish in Fort Wayne; and St. Martin de Porres parish near Lake Wawasee.

It meant a separation from Bishop William McManus, a Chicago-born bishop, who brought me back to Indiana when he was appointed Ordinary to Fort Wayne-South Bend and with whom I lived for seven years until he retired and returned to Chicago.

It meant a separation from the Galilean Church as I headed for Jerusalem. I wondered when I left for Chicago whether I was also leaving Papakeechie for good.

I am consoled by Jesus; as soon as he was freed from the tomb, he announced that he would return in haste to meet his apostles in Galilee.

On August 1991, three years later, I found myself back again at Lake Papakeechie. It was a dream world to me, as I savored each day of that two-week vacation. My friends Paul and Edna Bente offered me their cottage, just three doors down from where I formerly lived.

My tears were not intermingled this time; there were only tears of thanksgiving for God's wonderful providence in bringing me back to Lake Papakeechie. I was living alone in a quiet, retreat-like atmosphere, where I could work, go for long walks, pray, and meditate in peace, without the interruptions and distractions of Chicago.

What made my return to Lake Papakeechie very special was my own personal recovery from a stroke nearly two years before, on November 5, 1990. The Jerusalem Church had tried to put me to death. Escaping death, I returned, like Jesus, to Galilee.

I felt like the young Newman, who was taken deathly ill in Sicily, far from home and loved ones, but who was nursed back to life by the young Gennaro, who was his guide in Sicily.

Newman's feverish illness was a time of introspection. Weary of his struggle through the wilderness, he was at peace with God, because God was leading him. It was then that he composed his beautiful hymn, "Lead, kindly Light, amid the encircling gloom, / Lead thou me on! / The night is dark, and I am far from home. / Lead thou me on!"

I have been gradually recovering from my stroke, including a speech impairment and a writing handicap. With a great desire, I had wanted to come back to Lake Papakeechie to write again. And I was writing in longhand (four months before, I wouldn't have tried).

'Amid the Encircling Gloom'

AT first I was deeply depressed by the fact that I lost two abilities that were always my trademark and my source of ministry. First, I couldn't write, and secondly, I couldn't preach. Finally, even saying Mass was difficult. I had to learn it all over again, and my voice was so weak — not only could I not preach, but I couldn't make it through a public Mass, sometimes not even through a private Mass.

Once a priest-journalist is stripped of these three abilities — saying Mass, preaching, and writing — he is reduced to nothing.

In a split second, the Lord had leveled me.

Except from one special relationship which the Lord had prepared in advance, without my even knowing it, I didn't have too much to live for. The Lord had prepared a young Gennaro for me.

The one special good thing that has happened to me since my return to Chicago has been an eighteen-year-old black youth by the name of Tony. His friendship, which began shortly after I returned to Chicago, now over four years ago, had been even more rewarding since my stroke. It is as though Jesus had wanted to prepare me for my stroke almost the day I arrived in Chicago. Neither Tony nor I understood what it was about.

In January 1991, back from the hospital and with a long recovery ahead of me, I asked for an early retirement from the Archdiocese of Chicago. Normally, a retirement comes at age seventy, whereas I was only sixty-seven . Through an understanding with Cardinal Joseph Bernadin, I received an early "disability" retirement forthwith. As a retired priest, I moved into independent living at the Atrium Village, where only a year before I had established a Newman Center, as part of my work with the Friends of Cardinal Newman Association. Now I moved into the Newman Center, and this became my major work as a retired priest. The pattern was fixed.

I could now work with the Friends of Cardinal Newman Association and begin a slow recovery program, and I could keep my association with St. Joseph's parish, which was less than half a block away.

Enter Tony, whom I had met in the neighborhood some three years earlier when he was in the eighth grade. I was new to the North Side of Chicago when he volunteered to show me around. It marked a beginning of a unique friendship, which has grown deeper each day. But it wasn't until I had my stroke that the real Tony stood tall.

You can understand that when a celibate diocesan priest gets struck down with an illness at sixty-seven years of age, far from his relatives and friends in Fort Wayne, Indiana, he is concerned about who will look after him.

My brother priests in Chicago, with whom I had been dissociated for some ten years while I was in Indiana, and I had never had an initial close association. As a late vocation who studied in Rome and spent not a day in the local seminary system, I didn't have many living priest friends. My friends for the most part came from the lay world.

But along came Tony, his grandparents, and his mother, to look after me. Tony moved in with me to make sure I had a watchful eye on me. He drove the car for me, took care of errands, and nursed me back to health, primarily by not treating me as a sick person but demanding I not act like one. In turn, I kept him in a Catholic high school, paid for his tuition, books, and clothes, and fed him.

Raising a teenager took my mind off myself and gave me someone else to worry about. That was good therapy. Tony challenged me to resume some of our activities, like playing pool and gin rummy, going to a health club. He challenged me to help him with his homework. Helping him with his English assignments has been my greatest speech therapy.

What has this done for me? First of all, it has taken my mind off myself. I now have a teenager to take care of: to get him up for school, to cook for him — all the things you parents go through with a teenager. "Can I have the car tonight?" I haven't had time to worry about myself. Cleaning the apartment, shopping, and cooking have made up a part of my day.

Well, it was almost a year since my stroke. I was back at my old routine (except it took me longer to accomplish it) of writing, saying Mass, and preaching. I have been writing this book.

A seventy-plus lady stopped me recently and asked me how I kept so young. I leaned over to her and whispered in her ear, "Have a stroke." Well, she allowed she wouldn't want to go that far.

But the repercussions of my stroke are even deeper. Like many men caught up in an institution, whether church, government, corporate life, or whatever, I was a candidate for a stroke for several years. I was involved full-time in the institutional Church through an assignment with *The New World*, our weekly diocesan newspaper. I was active on the board of directors of the Catholic Press Association, and as executive director of The Friends of Cardinal Newman Association. I was active in St. Joseph's parish on the outreach committee.

My body finally gave out. I had never missed a day because of sickness for most of my life. I thought I could go on forever at the same pace since my ordination in 1965. My spirit was good, but the strain on my body had taken its toll.

Then the Lord reminded me, you'd better slow down. I was fifty-four when I came to Our Sunday Visitor, Inc., in Huntington, Indiana. I made trip after trip on special assignments to every country in Central America, to Poland, Africa, Thailand, Lebanon, and my energy seemed inexhaustible; but these journalistic trips to the Third World countries were exhausting. I should have seen it coming in Chicago, at age sixty-seven. I was fatigued, I had frequent sweats, my breathing was heavy, I was overweight, but I kept driving ahead. And then, in the blink of an eyelash, I was in the hospital.

'Lead Thou Me On'

ONE of my attractions to the priesthood at age thirty-seven was the Galilean spirit, as opposed to the Jerusalem spirit. In the last ten years I had also called it the Papakeechie spirit, which I often likened to Lake Galilee's. In Galilee, Jesus seemed most at ease with his disciples, as he went about his ministry up and down the hot and dusty roads of the Galilean countryside.

He seemed to reject everything about the Jerusalem Church — its priests and elders, its religious sects, its pharisaical attitude. Not a priest from the priestly sect himself, but rather a prophet, he accused the Pharisees of their hypocrisy. Eventually, of course, the Jerusalem Church put him to death.

I longed to get back to Galilee, to Papakeechie. At sixty-seven, I was disillusioned with the institutional Church, even though I realize that the Galilean Spirit can be present in the institutional Church, that some bishops or administrators are

Galilean at heart, but the bureaucracy seems to limit the Galilean spirit, to make it difficult to be Jesus-like in our actions.

But we need only cite Pope John XXIII, Archbishop Oscar Romero of El Salvador, Archbishop Raymond Hunthausen of Seattle, Archbishop Rembert Weakland of Milwaukee, Archbishop Paulo Arns of São Paulo and Dom Helder Camara of Recife, Brazil, as witnesses of the Galilean spirit. I could go on and on. And of course this can be extended to pastors and lay ministers. We can recognize the Galilean spirit in every walk of life. It simply means more concern for the needs of the people than for the structures of the institutional Church.

I am sure we can find the same spirit in government bureaus, corporation boardrooms, the military-industrial complex, and in a hundred other professions and businesses. Men especially, and even celibate men, get programmed into the corporate structure, and they begin to think alike and look alike, as they soon lose their nurturing spirit, their husbandry, the sensitive contacts with their family, most especially their children or, in the case of priests, the people they serve. They get further and further removed from a father image. Men become consumption-oriented.

But on my return to Chicago, I was thrust back into the institutional church. I had yearned for retirement at age seventy so I could get back to pastoral ministry.

Then it happened. When I was laid low with the stroke, I had the opportunity to retire from the Jerusalem Church and to give what time I had to ministering a teenage boy from Galilee.

Robert Bly, in *Iron John*, has written, "Not receiving a blessing from your father is one injury. Robert Moore said, 'If you are a young man and you're not being admired by an older man, you are being hurt. Not seeing your father when you are small, never being with him, having a remote father, an absent father, a workaholic father, is an injury.' "

I prayed this wouldn't happen to Tony. The stroke changed my priorities. I had retired from the corporation, the Jerusalem Church. I now had time and leisure to give to a teenage boy.

Bly adds, "Blows that lacerate self-esteem, puncture our sense of grandeur, pollute enthusiasm, poison and destroy confidence, give the soul black and blue marks, undermining and degrading the body image — these all make a defilement. They damage and do harm."

Tony is a national Judo champion. He has been doing Judo since he has been nine. Today he travels over the country to participate in Judo matches. He is dedicated. His *sensei* (teacher) is a sixty-five-year-old master. He has encouraged him and tutored him since he was a scrawny nine-year-old. Today he is preparing for the 1996 Olympics.

I have encouraged him in this activity. He gets affirmation from his *sensei*, his family, and me. I believe that Judo has helped him make a difficult passage to manhood. When he came home and announced that he won the coveted Black Belt, I embraced him and said, "Today, you are a man."

André, a black youth from Fort Wayne days, called me at Lake Papakeechie recently. We talked for over an hour. He is in his twenties now, but we had the same kind of relationship when he was fourteen and raised by his mother. Our friendship lasted four years in Fort Wayne, Indiana. I knew it was hard on him when I left for Chicago a few years ago.

That night we talked about everything. Not long after I left, he signed up for the Job Corps at Camp Atterbury, Indiana. In two years, he finished high school, learned the bricklaying trade, and took up barbering on the side.

He excelled in everything he did at Camp Atterbury and soon became the leader of the camp.

Now he is at Indianapolis, working in construction, goes to barbering college, and beyond that has conquered his anger tantrums, which got him kicked out of school in Fort Wayne. André is now a man, and we rejoiced in that. It was simply a matter of affirming him when he needed it.

Bly continues: "Never being welcomed into the male world of older men is a wound in the chest. The police chief of Detroit remarked that the young men he arrests not only don't have any responsible older man in the house, they have never met one." The recurrent theme I heard from André that evening is that I became a significant friend at that time of life. He unashamedly told me how much I meant to him during that difficult period in Fort Wayne. In a small way, as an older man, I made a difference in his life.

A man's spiritual pilgrimage begins in many ways, but mine began again with a disabling stroke. Once I realized this, and I retired, I had to start a new life. Sam Keen, in his *Fire in the Belly*, writes about the virtue of empathy, which marks the lives of those who have returned from the journey into the depths of self.

He writes. "In his manner of living, the philosopher Gabriel Marcel exemplified, and his writing described and gave a name to, this heroic virtue — '*disponibilité*,' which he suggested should be translated as 'spiritual availability,' or 'spiritual readiness.' It's easier to understand if we start with its opposite. The unavailable man is encumbered with himself. His preoccupation may take the forms of obsession with money, power, reputation, health, psychoanalysis, or even his 'spiritual journey.'

"Whatever the form, it renders him unavailable to give himself to others or live vibrantly. . . . The available person is not encumbered by his possessions, his self-image, and hence has the capacity to listen and respond to an appeal made by others of him. . . . He is porous rather than impermeable, animated by trust in the inexhaustibility of being."

Keen believes if you are not married, do not have children, you should find a friend's child who needs nurturing and become a part-time substitute parent.

'The Night Is Dark'

THE question remains, who holds the father when he is weak or weary, or in my case, affected with a stroke? Who will comfort a strong man when he loses his strength?

I tussled with this while on retreat in 1986, five years before I had my stroke. All during my retreat I had trouble with the idea of Jesus embracing me, but I couldn't get hold of why this idea turned me off. Then it began to come clear to me. I have no problem embracing Jesus (Tony? André?) but I resisted his embracing me. Why?

I saw nothing in Mark's Gospel (which was my retreat guide) where Jesus embraced his apostles, or where they embraced him. Jesus is the Giver — to his disciples, to the crowd, to those in need, to the five thousand hungry people. His heart is constantly giving itself away, being torn from him. That is his mission right up to death on the cross.

But Jesus doesn't seem to receive from another. He doesn't allow others, not even his intimate disciples, or Joseph and Mary, to possess him, respond to his needs — except the Father. Is there a wall around his heart that doesn't let anyone get too close to him, literally, to possess him? He doesn't possess or allow himself to be possessed by another — except the Father.

I may have to go to St. Paul to resolve this problem. Paul seems totally possessed by Jesus. "Not I but Christ lives in me." "Dissolved in Christ." A total madman for Christ — possessed.

Pope John Paul II also is a man possessed by Jesus. "*Totus Tuus,*" he kept repeating over and over when I followed him in Poland. "All is yours."

Looking at my own life, I enjoy being the Giver, but I resist being the Receiver. In 1986 on retreat I asked that I could more fully give my life to others, be more generous in my love, more detached from my time, space, gifts, material things, in order to share them with others. All noble prayers. But still I don't allow others to give to me. I don't ask. I back away from gestures of gift-giving to me. I have a kind of private part of my heart. I let no one in. I am afraid to appear vulnerable and dependent.

There is a part of me I keep to myself and am afraid to be open with others. I am afraid of an embrace from another, and so the embrace of Jesus, unless, of course, the initiative comes from me. With my spiritual sons, I enjoy giving to them. I love them. But I am the Giver, almost as if they are on spiritual welfare. Is this why I am attracted to inner-city kids? Have I spoiled them by not letting them love me in return?

So my reflections went in 1986, more than six years ago. It is simply that I had difficulty allowing Jesus to possess me, even though I wanted to possess his heart. "Rest in the heart of Jesus" is no problem, but to let Jesus embrace me, I am no longer in control. I lose the initiative.

But now it was 1992. I have since been wounded with a stroke. I am no longer a strong man. "Who nurtures and comforts the strong man when he is hurt and weary?" Who tends to the wounded healer?

The first six months after my stroke, I couldn't pray. My life as a Giver was decimated. I became a Receiver. It was difficult. I could speak only with difficulty. I found the Mass, after three months without attempting it, a struggle. I couldn't preach or even read the Scriptures. I couldn't fathom the Breviary. I was on spiritual welfare as well as on public welfare.

And eventually, I came back to health. I began to pray — the Mass and the Breviary, read Scriptures, and now books. I began to write, although it has been a real struggle. Once back at Lake Papakeechie, I began to commune with nature, take long walks in the woods, and regain my love of solitude.

It took me five years and a disabling stroke to finally embrace Jesus. Like Jesus in Gethsemane, I was now on my knees totally face to face with the Father, and I cried out to him. Even my most intimate friends fell asleep. Now I was asking him for help. My active days of helping others were winding down. But as the Father helped me, so I began to reach out again to Tony, this time in a different way.

Now I became a husbandman nurturing him, as any father or older man should. Keen writes: "The image is central to gay men, bachelors, and widowers living in high-rise apartments as to married or landed householders. Psychologically, the husbandman is a man who has made a decision to be in place, to make a commitment, to forge bonds, to put down roots, to translate the feeling of empathy and compassion into an act of caring."

It was like a joy coming after a long depression. A sense of joy and enthusiasm returned to me. It was my Second Spring, in the famous words of John Henry Newman. "Man rises to fall. He was young, he is old, he is now young again. He is born to die." The long dark night of the soul is over.

Keen, after his journey into his soul, writes, "Maybe I am okay just as I am. Maybe I didn't have to do anything to justify my existence. Maybe I don't have to strive anymore. Simply, gratitude for the gift of life."

'Lead, Kindly Light, Lead Thou Me On'

IT is a year later, to be precise, the summer of 1992. I am back at Lake Papakeechie; this time I have rented a small cottage year-round. I will spend several days in Chicago each week, but my base of operation is my beloved Lake Papakeechie. I am putting the final touches on this book. In another year, after I turn seventy years old, I hope to retire here.

Indeed, *'Lead Thou Me On' : Reflections from Lake Papakeechie*, the title of this book, is tied up with Lake Papakeechie. It is basically a bringing together the "Perspectives" and other articles I wrote for *Our Sunday Visitor* between the years of 1978 and 1992. It is really the story of my spiritual journey as both a priest and as a journalist; as a boy who left the farm outside Fort Wayne, Indiana, after high school, whose journeys took him to Chicago as a journalist; who became a priest of the Archdiocese of Chicago at age forty-one, spent twelve years in inner city pastoral work in Chicago, returned to *Our Sunday Visitor* for ten years as editor-in-chief, some ten miles from where I grew up on a farm, then back to Chicago — and hopefully now back to Lake Papakeechie for my final years.

This my story. My Apologia.

PART ONE:
Journal of a Wounded Healer

The Road to Rome

WITHIN an hour after the Alitalia flight touched down safely at the new Leonardo da Vinci Airport in Rome on the evening of October 6, 1962, I was on my way by taxi to the Pontificio Collegio Beda, a seminary for delayed vocations to the priesthood. It was a lovely Roman evening as the moon shone brightly overhead. I leaned back in the cab to enjoy the long ride into the city.

As we rode along in the silence and darkness of the evening, I thought about Rome — Rome, the city of Caesar, Cicero, Vergil, Livy, and Quintilian, whom I had just recently studied in a concentrated Latin course at Loyola University in Chicago; Rome, the center of Catholicism, the Catacombs, the Colosseum, the Forum, the Roman Empire, the long history of the popes and the ecumenical councils leading up to Vatican Council II, soon to begin in this eternal city.

I also thought of my own road to Rome, where I was now to begin my preparation for the priesthood at the age of thirty-seven. I recalled how, a little less than a year ago, the priesthood, Rome, a new direction in my life were far from my mind. Now I was on my way to the formal life of a seminarian at the Collegio Beda. With God's help, in three years I would be ordained a priest for the Archdiocese of Chicago. It was a lovely, reflective, somewhat lonely ride, but I was filled with gratitude to God for making these wonderful events transpire.

My own road to Rome, how did it come about? When friends of mine remark that surely I must have been thinking about the priesthood for a good many years, I am always somewhat embarrassed to confess that actually the idea was a recent one. True enough, as a small boy I used to play "saying Mass," for my mother had made some vestments for me, and I had a toy chalice.

Once I was in high school, the idea of becoming a priest never came into my mind. All through college and university studies, my one ambition was to become a journalist — a profession I was to follow right up to the very day I decided to become a priest.

Not only was I not called to the priesthood earlier in life, but I had very strong convictions about the lay vocation within the Church, an idea which took hold of me while I was doing graduate work at the University of Notre Dame in the late 1940s, where I came under the influence of Father Louis J. Putz, C.S.C., director of Catholic Action at Notre Dame and pioneer in developing specialized Catholic Action in the United States. It was through Father Putz that I became involved in the Young Christian Student movement, which, inspired by Father Putz, founded Fides Publishers, where I was to spend twelve years as Editorial Director in Chicago between 1950 and 1962.

Those twelve years were to become a rich apostolic experience for me in the Archdiocese of Chicago, not only with Fides Publishers, but in various forms of the lay apostolate, particularly the Young Christian Students, the Young Christian Workers, the Confraternity of Christian Doctrine, and in various other political, community, and interracial organizations.

In such a context of a deeply committed life to the service of the Church, my decision to become a priest came about. Conditions were such in the summer of 1961 for me to respond to God's call without too much difficulty. One year before, my ailing mother, whom I had been caring for, died unexpectedly from a stroke. Her death left me alone in a small house on the Southeast Side of Chicago. Professionally, my position with Fides Publishers was changing, for the company was consolidating all its activities at the University of Notre Dame. I was faced with the decision of either moving to South Bend, which meant leaving my commitments in Chicago, or finding a new source of employment. Also, at this time I was finishing a book, *Revolution in the City*, which would complete my activities in a racially changing neighborhood. I was searching for a new project to get involved in — and to write about.

With these various new circumstances in my life revolving in my mind, I enrolled in a workshop of the Confraternity of Christian Doctrine at Catholic University in Washington, D.C., in July of 1961.

While I was in the relaxed atmosphere of the university, far from my preoccupations in Chicago, one morning while attending Mass in the crypt of the Basilica of the Immaculate Conception, the thought of becoming a priest entered my mind for the first time. I tried to push it aside as something fanciful, fleeting, and also highly impractical at my age, for I envisioned a six- or seven-year seminary course, among fellows fifteen years my junior. The thought of resuming studies again and learning Latin frightened me.

Yet, as God would have it, in the evenings I would walk across the campus of Catholic University with a small group of Maryknoll seminarians, as we would say the Rosary together, discuss, and perhaps have a little party together in one of the dorms. A certain tranquillity came over me, and also a certain attraction even to life as a seminarian. Little did those seminarians know what was going on in my mind.

When the workshop ended, I returned to Chicago and plunged back into my everyday work. The idea of the priesthood never crossed my mind again until the end of the month, when I made a business trip for Fides to Detroit to see Father Leo Trese about a manuscript he was preparing for publication. After a relaxed day with Father Trese, during which we talked about his manuscript and his parish, I caught a train back to Chicago. On the train that night, the idea of becoming a priest took possession of me again, and I explored it from every conceivable angle.

When the train arrived in Chicago, one thing was clear in my mind. Tied up with the desire to become a priest was my desire to study for the Archdiocese of Chicago. The two ideas were inseparable. It was never a question of one or the other religious community, but a vocation to the secular priesthood in the city to which I owed all my apostolic experiences as a layman. I knew I had to resolve this problem. It was not something I could dally with any longer.

Within a few days I was seated in the study of Monsignor

Arthur Terlecke, the wise and experienced pastor of St. Gregory's Church in Chicago and a close friend of mine. At this juncture I wanted to talk to an older priest in the Archdiocese to explore the possibility of being accepted in Chicago. After discussing the matter by phone with various well-placed men in the Archdiocese, Monsignor Terlecke decided that I should take my case personally to Albert Cardinal Meyer, Archbishop of Chicago.

My brief encounter with Cardinal Meyer, one early August day in 1961, was the beginning of a personal relationship I was to treasure until his untimely death in 1965. I say this not only because he accepted me as a candidate for the Archdiocese and made all arrangements for my training at the Beda College in Rome, but also because of his warmth, kindness, sensitivity, and the encouragement he showed to a belated vocation. The memory of these brief personal encounters with him I carried with me on my ordination day, April 3, 1965, as he lay on his deathbed, no longer conscious enough to know I had reached my goal. He died six days after my ordination in Rome, and on Easter Sunday, April 18, 1965, I celebrated Mass for him at the tomb of St. Cecilia, in his titular church in Rome.

Albert Cardinal Meyer asked me only one question during our first visit. He wanted to now why I decided to become a priest. I told him simply that this was no hard decision for me, for I had made a dedication to the Church fifteen years earlier while a student at the University of Notre Dame. For fifteen years this dedication took the form of the lay apostolate. Now I wanted to make a stronger commitment, a rededication, a reconversion, if you will, to a total, complete, irrevocable life as a priest. I saw the priesthood as a culmination of events which had been set in motion fifteen years earlier. Beyond this, my vocation was a mystery of God's predilection.

Satisfied with my intentions, he began working out the practical details. Would I like to study in Rome? I knew little about the Beda College for late vocations, but I was thrilled with the idea. The Cardinal promised to explore the possibilities when he next went to Rome for some preparatory meetings for the Second Vatican Council. Meanwhile, I must begin studying Latin.

I asked for six months' time to get my house in order — that meant giving Fides Publishers three months notice, selling my house and its furnishings, finishing my book *Revolution in the City*, and disengaging myself from activities in Chicago. In the meantime I signed up for Father Laurence Henderson's intensive pre-sem Latin class for delayed vocations at Loyola University, scheduled to begin February 26, 1962. It was an intensive three-month course of thirteen hours a day, but I do know that the following October I was sitting in a big *aula* of the Gregorian University in Rome, listening to Latin lectures, taking notes in Latin, and doing oral and written exams in Latin.

And so it happened. One year from the first promptings by the Holy Spirit in the Shrine of the Immaculate Conception in Washington, D. C., to the setting down of Alitalia in Rome, those first hesitations, uncertainties, and doubts about belated vocations, those complicating problems of leaving home, job, friends, and commitments, and those fearsome Latin preparations were dissolved. In retrospect, none of it was as difficult as it sounds. Through it all there were those unexpected interventions of friends, priests, and bishops to ease the way. When God sets his eyes on someone for the priesthood, problems have a way of working out.

In Rome on the evening of October 6, 1962, I had the feeling that my past was now all behind me. A new life was opening before my very eyes, and I was filled with a certain satisfaction and calm of having had a general shakedown in life at age thirty-seven. Somehow I felt I was going to skip that much-feared boredom of middle age.

Priestly Influences

THE day I decided I wanted to become a priest, I turned to the assistant pastor in my parish in Chicago, Father Bob Carroll, who had become a very close friend through involvement in the Young Christian Workers movement. He had been my chaplain for three years. I was thirty-six; he was forty.

We went for a long drive in the country that day as I shared my aspirations with him. His support then, during my preparation for the priesthood, and after my return to Chicago as a priest, had a powerful influence on me until his untimely death in 1970. Father Bob taught me the meaning of loyalty to friends. He attended my ordination in Rome.

Before I met Father Carroll, another priest at the University of Notre Dame had a different kind of influence on me. Father Louis J. Putz, C.S.C., founding father of specialized Catholic Action in the United States (CFM, YCW, and YCS) involved me in Catholic Action when I was a graduate student at Notre Dame. He gave me a new dimension of the Church, especially the role of the layperson, and started all kinds of publishing projects. I worked with Father Putz for twelve years at Fides Publishers, a small book-publishing house he founded with a group of students in the late 1940s.

Even earlier on, still another dynamic priest, Father Syl Ley, C.PP.S., director of publications and professor of journalism at St. Joseph's College, Rensselaer, Indiana, made a journalist out of a starry-eyed farm boy. We worked side by side for four years in all kinds of journalistic experiences. Father Syl, now deceased, preached at my first Mass in Rome. By then he was in his seventies, but what a joy for his old age!

I speak about these three priests who unknowingly led me to the altar of God as an ordained priest, and they did it by close personal friendship. I can honestly say that not once did any one of them ever suggest or urge that I become a priest. They were faithful to me as a person who had an obvious journalistic vocation and who was deeply involved in the lay apostolate.

Once I made my decision, which came quite unexpectedly (and late in life), these three priests became my most enthusiastic support group and played an important role, each in his unique way, in my response to God's call.

For seven years, from 1978 until 1985, when I was in Fort Wayne, Indiana, the most important priestly influence in my life has been my roommate, Bishop William E. McManus of Fort Wayne-South Bend. This had not only been a bishop-priest relationship, but a priest-to-priest friendship, a man-to-man relationship, as we bached together as an "odd couple" in his small home in Fort Wayne — right down to doing our own cooking and "washing up," as the English call it.

Here we shared our hopes and dreams, our failures and our frustrations, buoyed each other up, and exchanged a lively sense of humor. We were casual friends in Chicago when I was in pastoral work there, but when he invited me to come to Fort Wayne and to *Our Sunday Visitor*, our close personal friendship blossomed.

My point is this, and I direct it to young men considering the priesthood: that priestly friendships are one of the unexpected consolations of the calling, and they are a wonderful support to the vow of celibacy. Our Lord has a wonderful way of taking care of his chosen ones. Unfortunately, these stories will never make a TV miniseries.

This much I can say. The four priest-friends I have just talked about were and are comfortable with their vow of celibacy. Two are now among the blessed: two are still among the living. Both living and dead serve as a beacon to me along the Lord's winding path to eternal joy.

Collegio Beda

MONSIGNOR Charles Duchemin served as rector of the Beda College in Rome for late vocations for thirty-three years before leaving in 1961. He died a few years later. On his twenty-fifth anniversary as a priest, Monsignor Duchemin was described in a way that gives insight into the kind of men he was dealing with at the Beda.

The Monsignor was called "learned but not too learned. He had the precious capacity for suffering even fools gladly. He was healthy, but not too healthy. He had that ready sympathy where physical ailments were concerned which is found in people who have had a taste of ill-health in their own lives. Finally, he was holy but not too holy. He had none of those priestly pieties so frequently confused with real holiness."

It was Monsignor Duchemin who so well understood the problem of a middle-aged man who wanted to become a priest.

Collegio Beda was first founded by Pius IX in 1852, under the name Collegio Pio. Father Francis Kirk, who came to the Beda in 1855, left this account of its inception.

"At that time there was a considerable number of Anglican convert clergymen preparing for the priesthood at the Collegio Romano and residing in their own apartments. The Holy Father did not approve of their living that way and desired they should live together in community. All of them expressed a desire to do so, but did not know how it could be arranged. The pope then took it into his hands and gave them a large suite of rooms in the Piazza Scossa Covalli, quite near to the piazza of St. Peter's; he appointed a rector and called it after himself, the 'Collegio Pio.'

"Within a short time the number of applicants increased so largely that it was found impossible to continue in our limited quarters. A proposal was made to the rector of the English College in the Via Monserato to allow an unused portion of the building to be prepared for our reception, while we kept our own rules as formerly and remained under a rector of our own."

This document was written more than one hundred thirty years ago. It was a time when the Catholic hierarchy in England had just recently been reestablished and when Cardinal Newman's lectures on "The Present Position of Catholics in England" were given. A number of distinguished Anglicans joined the Catholic Church, and some of them wished to become priests. Cardinal Wiseman advised Pius IX to found a special house for them.

In 1897, Cardinal Vaughan of Westminster spoke to Pope Leo XIII about developing Collegia Pio. By the end of 1898, when a *motu proprio* of Pope Leo sanctioned the constitution and rules, Collegio Pio became the College of St. Bede, the Anglo-Saxon saint, or Collegio Beda.

In 1961, when I was called to the priesthood at age thirty-nine, Albert Cardinal Meyer of Chicago sent me to the Beda. John XXIII College in Boston for late vocations had not yet opened, and the idea of a late vocation was not yet very current.

Late vocations are still an untapped source for vocations.

In looking at my ordination class, I immediately can think of two retired American Army Colonels, a former British Army officer, a former lay brother, a factory worker, an employee of the British transport system, several accountants, a sixty-nine-year-old retired New York lawyer (and widower with four children), an ex-Anglican priest, a retired farmer from Ireland, a Hyde Park Evidence Guild speaker, and a schoolteacher.

Or, if I think of my close friends at the Beda, I recall a convert German studying for South Africa who had spent five years in Siberia as a prisoner of war before escaping; a retired officer of the Indian Navy; a converted lawyer from Northern Ireland; a "First in Literature" from Cambridge; a schoolteacher, author of five books of archeological and historical interest; and a public relations man for Pepsi Cola in Latin America and Africa.

Their variety is endless, but Beda men are, on average, around forty years old (though ages can range from thirty years to seventy); in large part they are in the prime of life, with many years of service yet to give to their bishops.

The words imprinted on the Beda Coat of Arms tell the story: "*Christo spectante curramus.*" Literally, we are men on the run in search of Christ before time runs out.

Ordination to the Priesthood: 1965

A BEAUTIFUL ordination ceremony took place April 3, 1965, in the apse of St. Paul's Basilica Outside the Walls, Rome. Ameleto Cardinal Cigognani, protector of the Beda, imposed hands to confer the sacrament upon us. The simple but solemn ordination Mass was over by eleven o'clock that morning. It was so intimate that family and friends were practically in the sanctuary with us — they really had a close-up experience.

Immediately after Mass, I gave all my friends and family my first blessing. Then we went to St. Peter's for a special audience Pope Paul VI granted the new priests and their families.

Sunday, April 4, was the day of my first Mass (and what a

lovely, sunny day it was!) as about forty of us loaded into a bus to begin our thirty-five-mile drive outside of Rome to the little village of Castel Sant' Elia, near Nepi. Here was the church I had chosen for my first Mass — the Basilica of St. Elijah, which has stood since the sixth century. On the way out, we had a singing practice on the bus.

We arrived in Castel Sant' Elia, at the Franciscan monastery which has custody of the old basilica, by ten-thirty A.M.

In order to approach the basilica, which is practically inaccessible by car, since it is located at the bottom of a huge ravine, we had to walk down the side of a sloping cliff. After vesting in the monastery, we processed part way down the cliff to a shrine of Our Lady of the Rocks, where I intoned the *Veni Creator* as we began our solemn procession in song down the remainder of the cliff. What a breathtaking experience it was on that beautiful spring day! Finally, we came upon the ancient basilica and made a solemn entry into it, singing the Introit.

By one o'clock in the afternoon we were on our way, some five miles distant near Civita Castellana, to a fourteenth-century hunting lodge once owned by the Renaissance Pope Julius II, now converted into a picturesque *ristorante*, Val Sia Rosa, high on a cliff looking outward on Monte Soratte. We took possession of the lodge for the rest of the day.

Words can hardly describe the celebration at Val Sia Rosa. When our bus arrived, we were given a gun salute. When the flaming chicken was brought out, the place was darkened, firecrackers were set off, lights flickered. Then a wonderful clown, leading a six-piece local band, paraded in as the party really loosened up. When the cake was brought in, fifteen turtledoves were turned loose in the dining room, and as we departed a fireworks display was set off on the roof. Really, a celebration Italian style!

Monday, April 5, was another memorable day. I had long thought about saying Mass on this date in the catacombs for my deceased mother and father. We went deep into the bowels of the earth at the Catacomb of Priscilla on the Via Salaria, to the Greek altar, in a very small room where everyone was jam-packed around the altar for Mass. Here also I preached my first sermon on death and resurrection.

Tuesday, I celebrated Mass at St. Mary Major Basilica; on Wednesday, at the altar of St. Pius X in St. Peter's Basilica. By Thursday most of my friends had left Rome, as I celebrated Mass at the Beda for Albert Cardinal Meyer, who was dying in Chicago. On Friday Cardinal Meyer died, and on Monday there was a Pontifical Mass for him in Rome.

With all of my guests now gone, on Easter Monday I flew to Vienna, Austria, to spend ten days with my brother and his family and recover my strength. But a whole new experience awaited me in Vienna, my second home abroad — on Friday evening, a Mass at St. Josef's parish for the Young Christian Students and the Young Christian Workers, whom I had gotten to know so well.

Whitsunday was another big day, as we drove some forty miles out of the city to a small rural parish at Stelzendorf, in the heart of the winemaking country, for a Second Mass planned by Father Augustine Neudecker, pastor and friend of our family. The small rural community was all excited, for this was the first "First Mass" in their parish since 1899 — sixty-five years without a vocation! We had a wonderful Mass, with full participation, and afterwards a big Wiener schnitzel dinner and Benediction.

Then back to Rome again. The month of April 1965 will stand forever in my memory as a great blessing of God.

Castel Sant' Elia: 1966

THERE was never much doubt in my mind about wanting to return to Castel Sant' Elia, the remote hill town north of Rome where I had celebrated my first Mass, to observe the first anniversary of my ordination. Fortunately, the dates coincided with Holy Week, so I decided to go there to make a week's spiritual retreat. On April 3, the anniversary of my ordination, I boarded an autobus for the little village of Castel Sant' Elia, where I would live for a week with the Franciscan Fathers who had custody of the pilgrimage grotto for Our Lady of the Rocks.

After Mass on April 4, the anniversary of my first Mass, I spent several hours composing my retreat by retracing my steps of the year before this very date, but this time in solitude and quiet, free from all the excitement of a year ago. I spent a good deal of time inside the ancient Basilica of St. Elijah, where I had celebrated my first Mass, this time exploring every inch of this sixth-century basilica, savoring every detail of the sanctuary, the altar, and the fading tenth-century frescoes.

I walked down the long, winding path from the monastery to the ancient basilica, hidden away at the bottom of the ravine. Spring did not seem quite as far along as the year before: not quite as many buds were bursting forth; things were not quite as green; the air was a little nippy; but it was a lovely, sunny day on which to return. In the awesome peace and quiet there, amid the bursting forth of nature, I recollected myself for my retreat this Holy week of 1966.

Appropriately enough in this wildly naturalistic setting, I chose Pierre Teilhard de Chardin's *The Divine Milieu*, his own spiritual meditation, as my guide on this retreat. The view on high from the top of this ravine, where the monastery is located, looking out on the gaping divide below and Monte Soratte, was not unlike the horizons Teilhard must have looked out upon as a boy in France. Just as the Jesuit in his spiritual meditation divided life into the spheres of activity, endeavor, and development, and secondly into the sphere of passivity or what man undergoes, so I divided my retreat in terms of my own life in the past year as a student-priest in Rome.

As my spiritual inventory was to reveal to me the next few days, in the past year the emphasis in my own life had been more on passivity than upon action, as a student. Using Teilhard's test, I experienced more anxiety than joy over this situation. I didn't seem this past year to be building an "opus." Was I really putting any spiritual form into my soul? Was I bringing Christ to fulfillment, or rather, only a little fulfillment to Christ? In a word, I did not seem to be acting this year, unleashing any creative energies; there was no immediate end toward which I seemed to be working, no "opus." I seemed to be overcome with nothingness. In the past year my priesthood seemed to have withdrawn me from the ordinary ways of mankind, isolated me, diminished me. Had I become what Teilhard calls a straggler of the human race? Giving half of myself? Never experiencing the spurt or intoxication of advancing the kingdom of God?

The inventory of the "passivities" of my life this year in Rome revealed a leisurely year, free from any real academic pressure — after the previous years of intense, overburdened academic life in pursuit of the priesthood. It revealed more freedom — from seminary rules and religious exercises, not unlike the life I would soon be experiencing in a parish.

Then, the "passivities" of diminishment, or what I might call the humiliations of this year, perhaps better described as awareness of my limitations, that self-awareness best attained at middle age: failure to qualify for the license exam, a slowing-down of learning abilities, such as memory and language facilities; a few minor physical aches and pains — an awareness of advancing age but at a moment when I would hope to be at the very height of my powers. Finally, and most galling of all, a lack of pastoral outlets this year for my priesthood. In the confined atmosphere of studies, isolation from people, few liturgical and sacramental opportunities, no preaching, no real *cura animarum* for which I was ordained, lack of framework for leadership, scope for action, involvement. Thus a cumulative sense of a struggle against failure, all the more bitter at middle age and at the threshold of a new profession.

Until I returned to Chicago for a parochial assignment, there seemed no upward movement possible in these failures, except the consolation that they were temporary and that soon I would be projected back into an intense apostolic life in Chicago. So I must view all of this as a kind of purification, a death-to-self, until this year was over, that I might attain a more dependent relationship with God and union with him. I must try to transform these humiliations, make them a part of my spiritual growth, so that from this intellectual, moral, and physical death, I might rise again with new life. God was hollowing me out the past year, in Teilhard's words, in order to penetrate me more deeply.

Such were the main directions of my meditation, appropriately during Holy Week, as the Sacred Triduum approached. There was little I could do in face of all this emptiness and spiritual dryness but remain in silent prayer and composure and ask for some kind of miracle of grace, which seemed never to be refused me in this most holy place full of so much meaning for me in the past, the very place where I had begun my priesthood.

Nor was the grace to be refused me that week.

Castel Sant' Elia is a small peasant village north of Rome just off the Via Cassia. It stands nestled in, almost hollowed out of the tufa cliffs surrounding it, at the end of an enormous divide, in whose valley these peasants work their small farms. High on one of the divides is Santa Maria di Rupi, across the divide is Monte Soratte and also the town of Nepi. Between is a kind of fertile valley with a stream running through it, and here the *paisani* have stepped farms down both sides of the ravine. They come to their truck patches each day by foot or donkey, work all day, then return to the village at night.

Seated on the edge of the ravine meditating one morning, I thought of how much these busy peasants looked like ants far below as they went about their daily work this time of year preparing the ground, planting, trimming the trees of dead branches, as the women often hauled large bundles of dead wood on top their heads back to the village. How remote I felt from them, as remote as from the busy ants at my very feet going about their spring tasks. How little I knew about these people. How difficult it was for me to view them from such a distance as people with ordinary human hopes, joys, sorrows — and yet how ardently I desired to know them, for they were a vital part of this area which meant so much to me. In fact, the year before, many of the villagers had come down to the old basilica to attend my first Mass, and afterward it was a great thrill to give them my priestly blessing.

The Lord did not wait long to draw me into the intimate life of these people.

On Holy Thursday I ventured for the first time from the

cloister of the monastery into the village to mail some letters. On the way back I encountered two young boys who were soon to bring the village of Castel Sant' Elia to life for me. *Angeli Domini*. They were mending an old soccer ball and asked me for my help. One thing led to another as they became fascinated with this strange-speaking American priest, and we were soon having a language lesson. I tried to show them some basketball tricks with their old ball. We promised to meet again on Good Friday.

Quite unexpectedly, Good Friday evening I was invited, along with two of the Franciscan Friars, by the pastor of the village, Padre Domenico, to be the celebrant of a folk-liturgy torchlight procession through the village in memory of the dead Christ, an annual paraliturgical festival in many of these Italian peasant towns. It is a dramatic, funeral procession, at which the corpus of the dead Christ is paraded through the village, as most of the people join in. Much of the pageantry of the Cross is dramatized — a Simon of Cyrene carrying the cross, the women of Jerusalem in black hoods, Veronica with her veil; the village band playing mournful music, alternating with the singing of the people in procession; boys carrying torchlights, young men as an honor guard. Forming at the parish church (separate from the Basilica, which is never used), the procession winds through every street of the village and ends after several hours at the church again, where relics of the true cross are in exposition and where the statue of the dead Christ is venerated. We three priests led the procession dressed in full black vestments.

After the ceremony, the pastor invited me to return on Saturday to celebrate the Easter Vigil in the village church. Inasmuch as it was to be entirely in Italian, I had some hesitation, but I accepted. On Saturday afternoon my boys came to the rescue again — this time they helped me with my Italian pronunciations as I read through the lessons and orations of the Vigil Mass. Saturday night I would celebrate my first Easter Vigil as a priest, and in Italian! Surprising enough, everything went well, but *come modo Italiano*, which means not without a certain amount of confusion and chaos but still, I am sure, valid. The Easter Vigil Mass was to be my first Mass in Italian, including reading the

Epistle and Gospel. I imagine the people were quite amused by this American priest as he struggled with the language, but they were respectful and attentive through it all, evidently quite happy to have another priest in their midst — a rare occasion in their lives.

By this time I had been collecting quite a following of the young boys in the village, somewhat to the surprise of the people, as they saw their "new priest" followed through the streets by a straggling group of boys singing, chattering, and bouncing along. The boys and I were becoming fast friends, and I felt this was the first time they had ever had contact with a younger priest. They insisted on taking me on a pilgrimage down across the ravine on Holy Saturday afternoon to a huge cross high on the other side which the village had erected. Off we went on what was a delightful afternoon, romping with the boys in the warm Italian sun.

Easter Sunday I was invited to celebrate the eight A.M. parish Mass, again in Italian, and by now I was gaining confidence in my Italian reading. After Mass the boys were waiting for me, this time dressed in their Easter suits, to go off on still another pilgrimage to a grotto in honor of St. Athanasius hollowed out of one of the cliffs, which hung about half way up the ravine. I was certain the boys would get all dirtied in their Sunday clothes, but they insisted they wouldn't and proceeded to prove me wrong. After the grotto, we visited the old basilica, where they gave me all the history of it, then back to the monastery, where I bade them all a sad farewell. After dinner I was to catch a bus back to Rome.

From the emptiness and spiritual dryness which I had experienced earlier in the week, from the terrible feeling of remoteness from the village people, from the depression of not having any pastoral or liturgical experiences as a priest, I had come by Easter Sunday to a wonderful, almost exhilarating feeling of priestly vitality and joy. Like one of the buds on the bushes, everything had burst open for me the final days of Holy Week, and the village of Castel Sant' Elia became for me a beautiful spring flower. I had found my way into the heart of the village, and it is an experience I shall never forget. Now it seemed that everything about this area had been revealed to me, and I had a great priestly desire to come back to work among these people as their priest.

To what else can I attribute the events of this Holy Week, 1966, the first anniversary of my ordination, but to the miracle of grace, a miracle which I have become accustomed to expect, almost take as a matter of course, in this area not far from Rome where St. Benedict himself made one of his early foundations and where the pilgrim St. Benedict Labre encouraged a lay brother in the eighteenth century to hollow out a grotto to Our Lady? He spent eighteen years as a hermit carving his grotto of love out of stone on the side of the ravine. Today it is the Santuario Santa Maria di Rupi, a favorite pilgrimage place for the Italians, where miracles are expected as part of their simple life.

Return to Castel Sant' Elia: 1985

TWENTY years ago before on April 4, I celebrated my first Mass in the small, beautiful, ancient Basilica of St. Elijah, nestled in the hills some forty miles from Rome near Nepi. The village of Castel Sant' Elia numbers some two thousand people, a village I came to know well and love as a newly ordained priest. I returned there often to help out after ordination and during my last year in Rome.

On this recent visit to Rome, I returned to Castel Sant' Elia to see my friends of twenty years past. It was a grand and emotional return to the basilica of my first Mass and to the village.

Twenty years ago I had gathered up a group of *ragazzi*, ten-to-twelve-year-old boys, as I became a kind of pied piper in the village. I introduced them to baseball and barbecues and took long hikes with them in the area. On Sunday evening I would visit several of the homes for gigantic Italian meals. Some of the boys, like Fabio and Bruno, I came very close to. They became my Italian family.

When I arrived this particular Saturday evening, I came unannounced, but the word spread that Padre Vincenzo had returned — after twenty years. Within minutes our reunion began, and before the evening was over, we had a series of progressive parties in three homes.

I must confess I was apprehensive about returning. Fabio and Bruno would now have turned thirty. Would they still be there? What about their parents, now about my age? Would they remember this American priest of twenty years ago who spoke halting Italian, while they spoke not a word of English? Could I ever go back?

All my questions were dissolved in a few minutes. It seemed very little had changed. My first visit was to the small grocery store operated by Fabio's mother and father. I had enjoyed so many meals in their modest home above the store, as it seemed by the end of the evening most of the groceries, meats, and sweets came up to the dinner table from the store below.

Fabio's mother and father were working in the store, and they recognized me immediately. The mother hadn't changed much, but the father had been ill with diabetes and had lost a lot of weight. Within minutes Fabio and Bruno arrived — now full-grown young men, both of them married to attractive young Italian women from the village. Bruno and his wife had their first child.

Across the street and down a half-block is a photo shop with the name F. Branca in bold letters. My Fabio is now a photographer and has his own business. Bruno has a fine job in Rome and commutes every day.

The boys got a key to the basilica from the mayor — it is now under state care as a historical church, and much renovation has taken place in recent years. We visited the church of my first Mass. Another emotional highlight of my visit.

I stood in late evening on the balcony of Fabio's house, overlooking the village. How little life had changed in twenty years! The families were still intact and in close union. Life continued. It was as though I had never left. All the varied experiences of my twenty years as a priest flashed across my mind, and yet here was I at the very place where my priesthood had begun. The local parish still has the same pastor. I wondered if the Second Vatican Council had touched this village so close to Rome, and I judged probably life is not much different.

Padre Vincenzo had returned to Castel Sant' Elia and we had a wonderful time of it — a highlight of my visit to Rome, the Eternal City, where everything is possible and time never seems to run out.

Baptism by Fire: 1966

REFLECTING back on twelve years of pastoral experience in the black community (1966-78) on the West Side of Chicago, I am reminded of St. John's Gospel. Thomas, one of the twelve apostles, said to Jesus, "Lord, we don't know where you are going. How can we know the way?" Jesus replied to him, "I am the way, the truth, and the life."

When I answered the call of the Lord to the priesthood, some six years before at the age of thirty-seven, the Lord had already formed me — but without my knowing where he was leading me.

Like Thomas, I didn't know the way when he took me from the farm in Indiana at the age of twenty-five to the big city of Chicago. I didn't know where he was leading me, nor where I was going those twelve years in Chicago when I labored as a layperson in journalism with Fides Publishers, in community work in the racially changing neighborhood of Chatham, or in youth work with the Young Christian Students and the Young Christian Workers during the 1950s.

With Thomas I said, "I don't know, Lord, where I am going? How can I know the way?" Then suddenly, through his amazing grace, the Lord said, "Drop it all. Stop where you are in mid-life, and come, follow me." He led me to his altar as a priest at age forty-one.

Even during those four years of seminary training at the Beda College in Rome for late vocations, over and over with Thomas, I said, "Where are you leading me, Lord?"

And the Lord kept saying, "I am the way, the truth, and the life. That's enough for you to know. Come, follow me."

I remember when I received my first assignment in the mail, 1966, to Blessed Sacrament parish. I didn't even know where the parish was located. I had never been on the West Side of Chicago. I was far from home, in Rome, completing my theological studies. I had to look up Blessed Sacrament on the map.

Then how elated I was when I discovered it was down the street from St. Agatha's parish, because I had heard of the great work being done at St. Agatha's among the black people. Now I finally knew what the Lord had in mind.

"Lawndale, my son," he said, "Lawndale. That's what I have been preparing you for all these years, and you didn't know what I was about." Now I knew, for Jesus is indeed the way, the truth, and the life.

It wouldn't take long, I quickly discovered, before I was back in the mainstream of inner-city life in Chicago. Blessed Sacrament parish was located for the most part in the black community; its elementary school was ninety percent black, and only a remnant of the aging white families remained on the south end of the parish across from the Burlington tracks. Meanwhile, a Mexican-American community was fast developing on the southeast end of the parish.

The church itself stood at the boundary line along Cermak Road between the black and the white communities, soon to be black and brown.

I remember arriving at Blessed Sacrament on July 4, 1966, to begin what would become a twelve-year pastoral experience on the West Side of Chicago in the Lawndale community — six years as associate pastor of Blessed Sacrament, and six years as pastor of Our Lady of Perpetual Help parish, even deeper into the heart of the black ghetto.

It was the summer of 1966. Dr. Martin Luther King, Jr., had brought his civil rights movement to Chicago, and he was planning peaceful, nonviolent marches for open housing through all-white Cicero, which practically bordered on our western parish boundaries. Dr. King was living not far away, on Sixteenth Street.

I arrived at Blessed Sacrament on July 4. On July 13 Chicago experienced its first civil disorders, and the West Side burned down.

July 12, 1966, was a hot day in Chicago. Black youngsters were playing in water from an illegally-opened fire hydrant when two police officers arrived at the scene and closed the hydrant. When a youth turned it on again, the police arrested him. A crowd gathered, and sporadic window-breaking, rock-throwing, and firebombing lasted for several hours. The riots broke out again on July 13. Before the police and the national guardsmen managed to restore order, scores of civilians and police had been injured. There were 523 arrests, including 155 juveniles.

What were the terrible hurts and frustrations and anger in these black youths to cause them to burn down and loot their own neighborhood? These questions burned in my heart. I must find out. I committed myself to the young people of Lawndale.

I don't know, Lord, how many times I have had to start this youth work business all over again. I wasn't prepared to start it then.

I had quit youth work at age twenty-five because I thought I was too old to work with young people, but then I got involved with Father Putz, the YCS, and the YCW. At age thirty, I quit youth work again. "How can I relate to young people," I asked, but the Lord sent a talented young Korean war veteran, Peter Foote, into our movement, and I told the Lord, "Here is a young man worth giving five years of my life to," and I did. Peter went on to become the president of the Young Christian Workers in Chicago.

When I was thirty-five, my little bungalow on Maryland Avenue was overrun with young fellows from the streets of Grand Crossing. A social worker by the name of John LaMotte was assigned to our neighborhood, which was just beginning to experience racial change. John kept picking up young people off the streets and dumping them at my home. "Here, take care of them. Do something for them."

At age thirty-seven, I was called by the Lord to the priesthood. Now my youth work is surely finished, I thought. The Lord won't call me to it again.

Then, on that July day on the West Side of Chicago, at the age of forty-two, during my first days at Blessed Sacrament as a priest, I got the message again. "Go and work among the youths of Lawndale."

I spent the rest of the summer of 1966 quietly getting oriented to my role as a priest in this community. Already plans began to formulate in my mind for reaching the youth.

Our own parish community was probably four percent Catholic. Since the parish facilities were built in the days when the community was predominantly Catholic, they are substantial facilities. They can and should be used now in the services of the community to show the Church's concern for the community at large, especially the young people.

The presence of dedicated priests, sisters, and seminarians in all these programs is genuine Christian witness to our concern for the poor and the dispossessed. With the help of government funds and cooperation with the governmental and private agencies, the Church is able to get back into the stream of the inner city, to offer programs and services which it could never undertake by its own meager financial resources in these inner-city parishes. It helps define the new function of the Church in the city, not simply to prevent civil disorders but to be concerned with the needs of the community and to place itself at the disposal of the community.

In short, we felt we could build an effective apostolic movement among our black youth on the foundation of their summer experiences. The consequences were far-reaching, not only for the future of our parish but for the Church and the community.

Youth Ministry in the Ghetto

WHEN John Cardinal Cody sent me to Our Lady of Perpetual Help Vicariate, deep in the heart of Chicago's West Side black ghetto, as "Priest in Charge," I knew I was being sent to an assignment where angels fear to tread. Several white priests had been literally run out of the parish ahead of me — the last one remained only about ten days before his keys were taken away from him in the dead of night by an angry group of parishioners.

This was the year 1972. I had finished six wonderful pastoral years in the parish.

Does this make me some kind of pastoral genius? Not at all. The credit for my staying power in what was then the smallest and poorest parish in the huge Archdiocese of Chicago and of our beginning steps to make this parish — "the stone the builders rejected" — the cornerstone of the West Side should go to the young people who teamed up with me to make this a youth parish with a youth ministry. I am speaking of a team of young black high school, college, and professional students — all members of the Black Christian Students movement — who came with me to OLPH and let the people know we would be working in and among and for the black community.

Let me back up a few years to give the genesis of the idea. At the end of the Summer of 1968, I took some fifty black high school and college students to the Midwest Convention of the Young Christian Students at St. Joseph's College, Rensselaer, Indiana, where our group was joined by some two hundred fifty white students. In the course of the convention, it became obvious that the Young Christian Students, a specialized movement I had long been associated with, was predominantly a white, middle-class youth movement and had little to say to our black youth from the inner city of Chicago. Out of the convention, the Black Christian Students was formed, not segregated from the YCS, but a further specialization. "Like to like," as its founder, Canon Joseph Cardijn, would say.

Our black youth returned to Chicago convinced they had to develop their leadership potential, address themselves to the unique problems of black youth, and begin their own programs for black youth. The work that was begun in 1968 progressed quietly but steadily in Chicago. We were based at Blessed Sacrament parish in Lawndale, my first assignment as a priest.

When the call came to me to move ten blocks down the street into our Lady of Perpetual Help, the Black Christian Students were ready for the challenge. The leadership core was well formed — most of the early leaders were now in college or about to enter professional life. They came with me to OLPH.

Our Lady of Perpetual Help was a small parish, with some thirty-five adult families, a small school of one hundred eighty students, and a dynamic black nun, Sister Marilyn Hopewell, as director of liturgy and religious education. The people were tired of all the infighting that had gone on. They were ready for some pastoral leadership. When we announced that we were going to try to address the parish to the young people of the community and hopefully make it a youth parish of the West Side, the people were turned on. They had struggled long and hard for survival. They were tired. "Let the youth take hold," they told me. "We will support them. If they are working for our children, they are working for us."

I formed a youth team of ten college students who met with me regularly on what the parish should be about. We turned an empty convent into the headquarters of the Black Christian Students. Through assistance from Model Cities and the Catholic School Board, we developed a tutoring program for elementary children in reading, math, and black history. We located the offices of our ongoing Student Employment Service, an effort to find jobs for youth, especially during the summer, and our service of academic counseling, to help high school students choose a college and get proper funding, in our convent. We opened it all with an open house.

The three programs — Employment Service, Tutoring, and Academic Counseling — continued through the summer when we expanded our Summer Enrichment Program, which was to be partially funded by the Neighborhood Youth Corps of the Catholic School Board, Model Cities, the Department of Human Resources, and a grant from the Campaign for Human Development. By the end of the summer, we could point to four hundred jobs for high school students and college students to operate our West and South Side programs.

Under the direction of Sister Marilyn Hopewell and our music director, the Cornerstone Concert Choir was organized and began performing. Composed of some forty high school students, the choir sang on the third Sunday of every month at the Youth-Family Mass in the parish.

What has all this got to do with a youth ministry? A whole lot, we thought. We believed in small Christian communities. We believed young people would begin to center their lives in our community and our little parish, once they saw we were genuinely interested in black youth and willing to give them a full share in the responsibility of developing parish programs addressed to the hard-core needs of young people in the ghetto.

The Fall of 1972 was the beginning of a wonderful six-year love affair between myself and the people of Our Lady of Perpetual Help.

We were sending forth a group of young men and women, and I feel good about it yet today. It was a group en route to the peak of their lives. You will continue to hear from them for the next twenty or thirty years, long after I am gone. They will have an impact on the Church in Chicago, and they will have an impact on the community, on Chicago itself. You will see them rising to become mayors, senators, and state representatives, business leaders, doctors, and lawyers.

This was our great experiment at Our Lady of Perpetual Help over those six years (1972-78). I was never too much concerned with the pietistic level. The contribution of our leadership team was in the community. They moved the parish outward. Along with this outward thrust, we had the tremendous supportive leadership within the parish of Sister Marilyn Hopewell and her work with liturgy and religious education of our children.

Our parish was small, but wonderfully alive and dynamic. I want to thank all the people of Lawndale, and here I am going back fifteen years, for making a priest out of a man. I may have had all the proper seminary training when I arrived in Lawndale, but the people made a priest out of me. They gave me the equipment everyone on the West Side must have in order to survive.

What did the young black people teach me? You taught me how to get out into the streets and wheel and deal and fight for the rights of the black people to deal with institutions. You taught me how to be a white priest in a black community, how to be a liaison, a pipeline, a connecting rod between the white power institutions and the poor and needy in our midst. You taught me how to get the programs, the funds flowing back and forth, and how to get the doors open, so you might walk through them.

You taught me to be open as a person and that there are no clean-cut answers to life. You also taught me that there are no evil people, that everyone is a beautiful person, that people can be reached, and that the priesthood is basically and essentially getting tangled up in people's lives, in their needs of jobs, housing, scholarships, education, legal aid, counseling, or whatever; to get deeply involved in their lives on a personal level, because the needs of the poor press down upon us, steadily, day by day, hour by hour, and meanwhile the system from the outside grinds us down and demeans us.

You taught me patience — to tolerate patiently the abuse of the system, because the abuse of the system meant long lines and red tape and endless bureaucracy, and the endless delay the poor must experience in order to obtain even the most elemental things of life.

You taught me not to fear anything but fear itself. You taught me to live in this area, like you live here, barricaded with bars and double locks; to live here under the threat of violence and break-ins, among junkies and drug dealers, pushers and users; to live here as a man and as a priest, alone.

You taught me that black is beautiful, that young people are black, and beautiful, and gifted.

I thank the people of Lawndale for making a priest out of a weak man coming into this community, a reed bending in the wind. You made a priest out of a man. And above all you developed in me a spirituality that is grounded in the right attitudes about the needs of the poor, a spirituality based on involvement with the poor.

The Agonies and the Ecstasies

THE priesthood is neither as romantic as Bing Crosby's portrayal in "Going My Way," nor as agonizing as Richard Chamberlain's caricature in "The Thornbirds." It lies somewhere in between.

As I reflect on thirty years plus of priesthood, I would like to recap my own personal agonies and ecstasies.

First of all, the agonies.

Period one represents the first twelve years of inner city pastoral work in Chicago (1966-78).

In July 1966, my first assignment, I watched the West Side of Chicago burn in a civil disorder touched off by Martin Luther King's marches in Cicero. I saw the frustration and the bitterness of the black community over racism in Chicago.

In April 1968, once again the anger of the black community: the murder of Martin Luther King resulted in turmoil in the streets of Chicago. The hopelessness and frustration of black youths deeply moved me on both these occasions, as I witnessed their suffering and powerlessness in the ghetto.

The struggle of holding a small inner-city parish together with baling wire; approaching the Archdiocese of Chicago hat in hand to beg enough subsidies to keep the parish and the school open one more year. The endless hours spent in fund-raising activities — two bingos a week, direct mail campaigns, social events, constant begging for survival. The agony of living on welfare.

Living alone in an inner-city rectory, subject to weekly break-ins, personal danger, constant vandalism, and finally, a near emotional burnout. Experiencing the poverty of my community — rat-infested housing, slum landlords, endless hours in welfare lines, unemployment, sickness, mental breakdowns, courtroom trials, survival amid inadequacies to change the system.

The next ten years as (1978-88) editor in chief of *Our Sunday Visitor* have had these agonies:

Visits on assignment to refugee camps in Thailand, Africa, Poland, Austria, Central America, Mexico, Lebanon link me to the sufferings of refugees worldwide. I saw the horrendous plight of the refugee and dislocated, for the most part run out of their own homelands because of violence, oppression, civil war.

Had I not lived in the black ghettos of Chicago for twelve years, I could not have understood the almost identical struggle of those living in ghetto camps around the world. The same suffering, hurts, dispossession, alienation, and dependency upon welfare exists in Chicago as in the refugee camps. The poorest of God's poor, and for the most part (except in Poland) they are non-white.

If I made any errors in political judgments about the turmoil in various areas of the world, I pray those errors have been made on the behalf of the poor. If so, I will always have a good conscience about that.

The poor and the dispossessed have very few advocates in the media, simply because the media are by and large the creatures of special interests. If the Catholic Press fails to be an advocate of the poor, then its existence ought to be seriously questioned.

And now, the ecstasies of the priesthood as I have experienced them, by far outweighing the agonies:

The summer of 1966 was the beginning of a wonderful twelve-year love affair I had with the people of the West Side of Chicago. I will never forget the moving and beautiful liturgies we celebrated week after week in our small black parish, which became a sign of hope on the West Side.

All I can say today is, "Thank you, Lord, thank you for the understanding heart you gave me here as you gave to Solomon. Thank you for the buried treasure, the pearl of great price I found on the West Side of Chicago. Thank you for the companionship of the holy women of these parishes, and for your young people, and above all, thank you for those who have been closest to me — the youth ministry staff.

The ten years I spent with *Our Sunday Visitor*, my greatest source of joy has been the faith, generosity, and confidence of our readers. The response of more than five thousand readers to our Turkeys-for-Poland campaign, which raised more than a hundred thousand dollars for Catholic Relief Services, was beyond our fondest hopes, as was your help in distributing a quarter-million

Prayer for Poland cards to raise money for Polish refugees.

When I invited you to write a "Letter to Dawn," who had suddenly lost her husband, or when I requested your thoughts on joy, friendship, and loneliness, again your response was overwhelming.

Or how can I forget your response to various charities in Central America and Lebanon, especially Father Fabretto's orphans in Nicaragua, or help for Cambodian and Laotian refugees, Polish refugees in Vienna? And who will ever forget Juanita, the little Mexican doll who raised nearly fifty thousand dollars for the victims of the earthquake in Mexico City. I came to you as a priest and a journalist, and you shared yourselves fully. These have been high points of my priesthood the ten years I was with *Our Sunday Visitor*.

Finally, your generous involvement in The Friends of Cardinal Newman Association, to help us promote the canonization of this saintly religious writer and thinker has been an ongoing adventure. In 1991 Newman was declared Venerable by Pope John Paul II.

And so I have had two loves in my lifetime as a priest. The first twelve years was an affair between myself and my parishioners in Lawndale of Chicago. The next ten years, it has been with the readers of *Our Sunday Visitor*. The world is my parish.

Our journey has not ended yet. I am reminded of the story of the disciple who complained that the road was rough and difficult. The Buddha responded to him, "Friend, the road is long and difficult because you are trying to reach it ahead of time. The true purpose of the road is not to reach the end, but to make the journey."

On Being Called Late

SOME may question whether or not my experiences in twenty-five years of priesthood have been priestly, or whether I could have achieved all this as a Catholic layman. Am I a secular

49

humanist, or a priest? as my ultraconservative friends would phrase it.

What is the priestly character of social action, the inner-city apostolate, or even editorial duties at *Our Sunday Visitor*, or the *New World* in Chicago? How did all this differ from my life as a lay editor at Fides Publishers just before I entered the priesthood? Or my Catholic Action work?

These are not facetious questions. I have asked them of myself many times. I can only answer that Our Lord called me to the priesthood. The Church ordained me as a priest, and my bishops have given me the assignments I have had. The Spirit has worked through the Church in every point of my life.

What turns my life would have taken had I remained a layman is moot. I'll never know, but I can look back on twenty-five years of priesthood with thanksgiving, joy, continual praise to God for his graces and blessings, new friends and associations, and hopefully, a small amount of good works.

I like to believe my life has been enriched by the varied experiences the Lord has brought my way as a celibate priest fully committed to the service of the Church. I may not have survived outside the priesthood, given my own human weakness. It was the Lord's way of helping me along the path to salvation — merciful Lord that he is.

The journey has not ended.

Late vocations, I truly believe, are a different breed of priests, or why else were we called so late in life? We often don't quite fit the traditional mold of priests, in the sense that we have been shaped more by the secular world than by the Church or the clerical world. We seem more at home in the secular world than in the ecclesiastical, and the Lord usually finds a way to use our gifts in the secular world. Our roots in the Church are different.

In reflecting on my own calling as a priest, I have been rereading one of the first books Fides Publishers issued when I was editor, *Priests Among Men* by Emmanuel Cardinal Suhard, Archbishop of Paris, written in 1949. Although Cardinal Suhard was pre-Vatican II, he had a great influence on Pope John XXIII, who convened the Council.

Cardinal Suhard raises the question of the split between the priesthood and the real world. He agonizes over the fact that the greatest part of a priest's ministry is devoted to the body of the faithful.

"Aside from the Eucharistic Sacrifice and Baptism, should the functions of the priesthood, that is, the administration of the sacraments, preaching, common prayer, parish activities, and catechetical teaching, be performed solely with respect to the Christian people?" Or, "Should the sacramental emphasis be waived in favor of evangelization . . . briefly, should the priest today be a minister of the sacraments or an apostle?" Questions we are asking yet today in the decline of priestly vocations.

Well, my assignments as a priest called later in life have been more apostolic than sacramental. I know the past twenty-five years, for example in the inner city in Chicago (two percent Catholic) and then in editorial work, I have had relatively few sacramental experiences, such as weddings, funerals, confessions, even liturgies with more than a hundred attending, outside the celebration of the Mass and baptisms. On the other hand, most priests find the sacramental ministry the mainstay of their lifelong ministry.

Cardinal Suhard believed a priest's life must be both ministerial and apostolic, but he adds: "Artisan of peace and minister of restlessness, apocalyptic wrestler and suffering servant, the priest is a riddle in society — a model and a scandal." I hope I have approached his definition.

Notes from a Retreat Journal

IT was an old beat-up retreat journal I had forgotten all about, until I discovered it recently while unpacking some books. Now, twenty-eight years later, it is interesting to see if I am still aware of the same priestly realities as then.

On January 6, 1964, the Feast of the Epiphany, I wrote the following in my notebook:

"Discussion today with my spiritual director. He commented

on St. John on loving our neighbor, as God loves us. How does God love us? Not by possessing us, for he has no need of us. He loves us creatively — he works good in us. So we should love our neighbor, creatively, do good for him. Work for the good in our neighbor. Create good in our neighbor.

"I found this helpful on problems of love for friends. I am always perplexed on how to love a friend in a fully human way, and yet not be so absorbed in the friendship that it distracts me from God, from others, from my ministry. What is the right balance here? Certainly, not to not love, not to not have friends, or deep personal involvements. Our vocation is to love.

"Looking back on personal friendships, have I always tried to so love them? Or have I been selfish in my love, exclusive, possessive? I am afraid I have been too human, too selfish, too hungry for love.

"So also let us measure our good works, our ministry. Do we try to possess others through our works, or are we disinterested, totally dedicated to drawing the good out of others by our good works? How selfish are we in our good works?"

As I reread these words, I find little has changed over the past twenty-six years as a priest. The tension is still there in dealing with close friends. We are told we need relationships to survive, that celibacy should not isolate us from relationships or intimate friendships, that we must love our people, not build barriers around our hearts, not close in upon ourselves to protect our celibacy. Celibacy is not a negative promise, but an opening to others. And so it should be. No priest today would doubt that from experiences alone. Closing in on self in a selfish, self-centered way can be devastating, not only to celibacy but to priesthood.

Yet the tension remains. It is difficult to have close intimate friendships and yet not be exclusive, not be possessive, not be jealous lovers. That is the human side of our nature. A vigorous prayer life and a vigorous pastoral life can help us resolve the tension.

My experience the past twenty-six or so years as a priest tussling daily with this problem tells me we must love the significant others in our lives for what they are, not for what they can do for us — or for the Church.

For me, manipulation of a friendship (to manipulate the other for a self-serving end, or even a Church-serving end) is the worst sin of all and the worst betrayal of a friendship or a relationship. It is the sin of Pedophilia. If we love others for who they are, as they are, or creatively try to empower them with our love and the love of God, then we will serve them and ourselves best. Such a relationship can be intimate, affectionate, and pure.

Counseling the Brokenhearted

THE role of the priest, or anyone for that matter, in counseling the brokenhearted is not so much by word as by presence. The person who is struggling through a broken relationship, or a broken marriage, or a broken heart, wants most of all someone to be there when needed, someone to be available, someone to be accessible, someone to be present.

Words tend to be hollow at these moments, not really to ring true or be consoling. Words are cheap. They are often pro-forma — what one expects to hear, but silence is golden and can speak louder than words.

The nonverbal is more important. The sharing of tears expresses a sensitivity. Tears are good and healthy. A priest should be able to cry, not in a whimpering way but in sharing with another his grief, sadness, hurt, and pain.

Tears cleanse the emotions, give a fresh perspective, flush out the hurt and anger and the bitterness. Tears console. There is nothing wrong about crying, especially among men. Men need feel no guilt in crying. I never trusted a man who could not cry.

An embrace, a touch, ever so gentle, is also important. The tenderness of touch is more reassuring than a fumbling of words. It is as if one takes on the appearance, the emotions, the sadness of the other. There is a rapport of hearts. "Give me an understanding heart, Lord."

Prayer is important both with the other person and apart from the other person. Prayer is binding. Prayer is bonding. Prayer brings the Lord into our presence as a third person. We are not alone.

The woman with the hemorrhage, in Mark's Gospel, reached out to touch Jesus. Just to touch his garment would be enough. Her faith was strong. And her faith cured her. The healing power went out from Jesus to heal her.

So must it be in brokenheartedness. We must reach out to touch Jesus and let his healing power come forth. Indeed, it will come, perhaps not as quickly as in the Gospel stories, but it will come forth in God's good time.

There is a process here, the Psalmist tells us. At first, there is sadness, shock, frustration, anger, perhaps guilt mingled with hatred. And this may be a lingering period of near death.

Then there is pleading, a pleading for reconciliation, a pleading for healing, for help — a pleading that comes from the deep recesses of the heart, full of sobbing and emptiness before God, perhaps even anger with God.

But at some point in time, the healing begins, the pain eases, and gradually the wounded person near death begins to come alive again. Life begins to have meaning again. The emptiness, the dryness, the loneliness, the aimless drifting begin to recede. New movement, new life, starts stirring. Things begin to work out.

Then comes the joy, followed by praise of the Lord. "I will praise you, Lord, for you have rescued me." "Oh, Lord, be my helper. You changed my mourning into dancing."

The priest witnesses the process. He identifies with its stages. He experiences the sadness as well as the joy, the pleading as well as the praise.

And so the role of the priest-friend or counselor is presence, availability, accessibility. It is empathy.

"Daughter, it is your faith that has healed you. Go in peace." The words of Jesus to the woman with the hemorrhage.

A Priestly Heart

PERHAPS the most difficult task of a newly ordained priest is to develop what I will call "a priestly heart." I say develop, because I don't think a priest receives "a priestly heart" on his ordination day, but he does receive the graces to form within himself such a heart.

Some may quarrel with me, in this age of the People of God, that what I am about to describe is not peculiar to priests, but should rather be called a Christlike heart, or a Christian heart. Well, I am addressing my remarks to newly ordained priests, and as a priest I think there are certain special qualities of heart all priests should strive for as a special trademark.

What I have leaned from pastoral experience is that a priestly heart must above all be vulnerable. We are vulnerable enough, human, without seeking to be. Vulnerability will be interpreted by the world as naïveté, softness, weakness, foolishness, and indeed it is, because we are best known as "Fools for Christ." What a beautiful compliment!

As priests engaged in pastoral ministry, we are going to be "put upon" and taken advantage of, by the person who is down and out on his or her luck, who comes to the front door of the rectory for a handout, or by the alcoholics, druggies, or street walkers, whose only recourse for survival is "Gimme a quarter, Padre, for a cup of coffee."

Precisely because priests are seen as vulnerable, we attract every kind of hustler and problem-stricken person. That is a beautiful tribute to the priesthood. All kinds of alcoholics, pimps, hustlers, con artists (they called them tax collectors and publicans in the time of Jesus) want to break bread with us, and I mean the contemporary meaning of the word bread — "Gimme some money, Padre."

Because we can't say no, because by our calling we see some good in everyone, we are vulnerable. Often as not, we are deceived, but a priestly heart does not grow cynical over bad experiences. If someone asks us for half our coat, we usually give it all away. It should be very difficult for a vulnerable priest to die a rich man, but he will for sure share the eternal banquet with Lazarus, the beggar.

A priest will also be vulnerable in his personal relationships. Almost by "priestly instinct" he will allow himself to get caught up in all kinds of personal relationships, male and female, out of the best intentions, but here too, he will let himself be open to use or manipulation, whether in counseling sessions or in the pastoral care to the troubled, the lonely, the divorced, the neglected, gays and dolls, who will put their trust in a celibate heart. His very vulnerability will be his strength, but it may also signal relationships that are not always in the best interests of priest or people.

I am saying that vulnerability means an openness to relationships that at times can result in unhealthy dependencies. The danger is to risk that delicate balance a priest must always strive for in personal relationships between pastoral care and excessive and absorbing involvement.

Yet, a priestly heart will take the personal risks rather than close in on self and become sheltered from all personal relationships, isolate oneself from people, deny friendships, erect barriers, and retire into "busy work" to remain aloof. By definition, a priest must reach out to others, be especially attentive to the cries of the poor and to those most in need of healing, compassion, and pastoral care.

Let's face it. To be loved by another, to be trusted, to be called upon in time of need, to be respected, to be compassionate, to change people's lives, to call others to goodness, are very human satisfactions, perhaps more attractive to celibates than to non-celibates, as well as very priestly qualities. It is difficult to be a "all things to all people" without at the same time wanting to be someone to a few people.

Such a balance requires the commitment of a Melchizedek as well as the wisdom of Solomon. As the Lord appeared to Solomon and said, "Ask something of me, and I will give it to you," so the Lord asks the same question of priests on ordination day.

Like Solomon, the priest must respond: "I am a mere youth, not knowing at all how to act. I serve you in the midst of the people whom you have chosen. . . . Give your servant, therefore, an understanding heart. . . ."

The Lord was pleased: "Because you have asked for this — not for a long life, nor for riches, nor for the life of your enemies, but for an understanding heart so that you may know what is right — I do as you requested." The Lord granted him a wise and understanding heart — a priestly heart.

Sacramental Fervor

THE sacraments, on the day of ordination, become the special charge of priests. Until that day, priests have been on the receiving end of God's sacramental graces, but now they share in this special ministry of distributing these powerful gifts to others.

Not only to give new life through baptism, but to celebrate the Eucharist, utter the healing words of absolution, join loved ones in marriage, and be present and active during sickness and death — these are and have been a powerful motivation all along the slow road to priesthood. Today all this becomes reality. May no priest ever lose the fervor of his first years of handling Our Lord in his sacraments. May it never become routine.

Our model for this sacramental fervor, of course, is the special patron saint of secular priests, the Curé of Ars, St. John Vianney, the humble peasant priest who ministered to the small peasant village of Ars in France for more than forty years.

A confessor whose reputation spread throughout France, an advocate of frequent Communion, a devout celebrant of the Mass, a powerful homilist and catechist — the Curé of Ars is a model for parish priests who once remarked: "A good priest, a priest after God's own heart, is the greatest treasure God can give a parish."

What a treasure he became to the people of Ars, but not without great suffering. A man of low esteem, slow at learning, late arriving to the priesthood, not very attractive, and unhappy with his first and only assignment to Ars, St. John Vianney nevertheless had that essential quality of priesthood: a zeal for souls. "You'll always find enough people to buy banners or statues," he once said, "but it is the saving of souls that ought to come first."

Single-handedly and stubbornly, through prayer, penance, self- flagellation, and an unrelenting attack on the moral evils of his day — taverns, drinking, dance halls, lewd dancing, and sexual promiscuity — he stuck to his mission. And in the end, he not only converted the peasants of Ars but became confessor to hundreds of thousands of pilgrims.

The last year of his life — this sickly, emaciated figure died at age seventy-three — over a hundred thousand pilgrims came to Ars to confess their sins and be close to a holy man. For thirty years he had spent eighteen hours a day in the confessional, celebrated daily Mass, taught a daily catechism class, and visited the sick. He lived in a small room, where he existed on a few boiled potatoes, less than three hours a day — from nine o'clock in the evening until midnight — then back to his cold, damp confessional in the parish church.

I don't know how many of us in this age of consumerism, TV, radio, and computers could follow in those footsteps, although this was less than one hundred fifty years ago. But the message to priests is clear today. A priestly heart, zeal for souls, and a love of the sacraments are still the basic needs of the people of God, as they were in France in the mid-1800s. No priest can go astray adhering to that basic formula for sanctity given to us by the Curé of Ars.

People will be attracted to such a priest, as they were attracted to St. John Vianney. Eventually, the dance halls and the taverns did close up in Ars, the people accepted and loved their pastor, not so much for the fire and brimstone — some called it Jansenism — he preached, but for the quality of priestly life he lived among them.

The Curé of Ars may not be too popular a saint today. For some, he was too strict, dogmatic, unbending, a "dictator of the Faith." For others, he was too bound to tradition, too simple in his homilies and catechetics.

Moot questions. What remains is the virtuous life he

exemplified. Peace, transcendent peace, practical virtue, honesty, sweetness, and charity were all his, and what is more, there was joy and happiness within him and above him. He remains a model for parish priests.

In 1925, John Baptist Vianney was canonized a saint, a patron of all parish priests.

PART TWO:

Reflections from Lake Papakeechie

A Holy Space

CREATING a vacancy for God — putting space between ourselves and our friends, between ourselves and our jobs or professions, between ourselves and our families — sounds easy, even romantic, but how do we go about it? How can we find this space where we can be alone but not lonely?

First of all, by "holy space" we mean space where we can withdraw in solitude to commune with God, whether through nature or in quiet, diffused prayer, or even through the unobtrusive presence of a special friend.

I am writing these words tonight in such a space, a place removed from my place of work and from my normal place of residence. I am writing from a cottage on Lake Papakeechie secluded in northeastern Indiana, some forty miles from home and from work. It is the quiet place I retreat to as often as possible and where I do almost all my writing. Tonight I am in a bright and airy study, comfortable with familiar artifacts and books about me, soft classical music playing, and seated at a big desk, writing with a pen.

The cottage has been a Godsend the past several years, an oasis to return to after wide-ranging trips abroad on assignment. It is secluded; very few people have my phone number or know the location. To me it is a "holy place," a "vacancy for God."

Does it solve the loneliness inherent in a celibate life? No way, no more than being immersed among people solves it, or being pulled apart by relationships. Holy space is not intended to solve problems of loneliness, but to provide space between ourselves and those "meaningful others" in our life. Holy space allows for a certain rhythm to our lives between moments of intense activity and moments of silence and reflection, a certain balance between the demands of others crowding in on us and our own personal needs in order to survive.

Somehow each of us must find some holy space in our lives or "make some space" in our routines. Our lifestyle will pretty much dictate how we work it out.

When I was an inner-city pastor in Chicago, I spent months without seeing green grass or flowers or gardens or sunsets or sunrises, but I found my holy space every Saturday morning when I celebrated Mass in the apartment of the Little Sisters of Jesus, who lived among the poor in my neighborhood on the west side of Chicago.

The simple apartment in a rundown tenement building in the area, infested with rats and roaches as it was, was an oasis. The Blessed Sacrament was continuously exposed there. In their simplicity and poverty, the Little Sisters had succeeded in creating some "sacred space" amid the poverty, noise, and suffering of the inner city. There was a peace and solitude there on Saturday mornings, a joyous coming together with the Little Sisters in prayer, reflection, contemplation, and talks around the breakfast table, a stepping back from the struggles for survival by the people of Lawndale.

In a word, it was a time of regeneration and renewal of the spirit often bent to the point of cynicism, with the oppression around us.

I am sure inner space, holy space, can be created in thousands of ways, from jogging to writing, from scrubbing floors to singing and dancing or playing a musical instrument, from reading to gardening to tinkering with a car, from fishing to sailing. Basically, I am inquiring about those activities, often solitary in nature, when we are alone with ourselves but not necessarily lonely, or even when we are engaged in something with a friend who places no demands on either of us, but only a kind of silent, mutually understood presence for each other as we do what we want to do.

These holy spaces are where we engage ourselves more in

being than in doing, in finding rather than seeking, in discovery rather than searching. There is an awesomeness about the element of surprise, the delight of a sudden new discovery, like stumbling onto a sunset or into a cold breeze. It is from these encounters with our hidden but ever present God that we can return to our human relationships with new fervor and delight.

Michael Rowed the Boat Ashore

DEAR Michael,

It was an emotional event for me, as I know it was for you, when I was able to pour the baptismal waters over your forehead during the Easter Liturgy at St. Mary's Church, Fort Wayne. To baptize you, to confirm you with the Holy Spirit, and give your first Holy Communion is a highlight of my priesthood.

You have been a very special convert to me, Michael, because of the friendship we developed over the past several months. When André, Carvin, Derrick, and you got into the car Easter Sunday morning and headed up to Lake Papakeechie for a celebration of your Baptism, my heart was overflowing. I recalled the words of Jesus on the day of his resurrection when he said he would meet his beloved disciples in Galilee. Lake Papakeechie has always been my Lake Galilee, and it is here I spent so many wonderful hours with my own little band of disciples in Fort Wayne.

And now you are one of them, a new member of the Papakeechie family.

This was your first visit to Lake Papakeechie. I know there will be many more. I was delighted to find out from you that you like to fish. All my disciples are fishermen, as were Jesus' disciples.

It was in Galilee that Jesus performed most of his ministry — his healings, his teaching, his reaching out to others. Galilee was where he was most at home, not Jerusalem. Jerusalem did him no favors, and it was in Jerusalem he was to die. How fitting, after his moment of glory, that he wanted to return to Galilee to be with his disciples! I felt the same way, Michael, on Easter Sunday. It was time to get out of Jerusalem and head for Lake Papakeechie.

We are Galileans at heart, more comfortable working the temple precincts, not hanging around in the temple; more comfortable with the outcasts than with the Pharisees, more at ease with the law of love than the code of law; more person-to-person, less structured and cultic. It was the Jerusalem Church that put Jesus to death, not the Galileans.

You are a new Christian now. As time goes on your faith will deepen and your knowledge of Jesus and his Church will expand. For now, you are a member of God's household, entitled to his inheritance, and you can call him Abba, as I hope one day you will be free to call me.

The fish weren't biting on Easter Sunday the few short hours we were there, but they will bite as the summer comes along, and you will catch fish, Michael, more than you ever dreamed of. And one day you will be a fisher of men.

I heard this funny story recently. It seems a man won a liar's contest, with this story line, "I met an honest fisherman." The comment on the lie pointed out the irony of the story that Jesus himself chose twelve fishermen to spread the truth of his teachings. It was as if he had the last laugh.

Some wonderful graces await you as a newborn Christian. I hope to be a part of some of them. Anyway, you have the pledge of my continued support. I am looking forward to being at your side the rest of your journey of faith. That may be a short time. You are seventeen, and I have already been a priest more than twenty years. But who knows?

In the Style of Jesus

THE next day John was with two of his disciples, and he looked at Jesus as he walked and said, 'Behold the Lamb of God!' Jesus turned and saw them. 'What do you seek?' he asked. 'Rabbi where are you staying,' they said. 'Come and see,' he said. They came and they stayed with him that day, for it was about the tenth hour. One of the two was Andrew, Simon Peter's brother. He went to his brother and said, 'We have found the Messiah' " (John 1:35-40).

I first met André at St. Mary's inner-city parish in Fort Wayne on a Sunday morning after Mass. I had been helping my good friend Father Tom O'Connor on Sundays during Lent. I always liked helping at St. Mary's because it reminded me so much of my inner-city work on the west side of Chicago. I so enjoyed working with the Black Christian Students in Chicago.

André had just turned fifteen and was a student at a Catholic high school. Father Tom has done a yeoman's job getting black students into Catholic schools. André was one of his protégés. A year ago André was baptized Catholic, after attending the RCIA program at St. Mary's. André and I had a long conversation the first Sunday I met him, and I instantly took a liking to him. On his birthday I took him out to dinner to celebrate, and I've kept in touch with him.

Recently I invited him to come with me to Lake Papakeechie to do some fishing. Also I had some yard work and spring cleaning I needed done to get the cottage ready for summer.

André asked me if he could bring his cousin Carven with him, and I said yes. André invited Carven, and one morning I picked them up at daybreak to drive to the lake. I had rigged two fishing poles and got a paddle boat from a neighbor for the day. They went fishing in the morning, and fortunately the fish were really biting. I had scouted out the lake the day before.

At noon they came in and I grilled some hamburgers and hot dogs for them. Then we finished our yard work and housecleaning. By four P.M. they were back fishing, and by eight P.M. I had them back home in Fort Wayne.

André asked me if I could give them a lift to a party. Out he came with Carven, and now Allen and Tony, two more cousins. By now I had a carful of four teenage boys.

"Where are you going to school?" I asked them.

"We want to go to a Catholic school next year," one of them piped up.

"How many are Catholic?"

"Just André."

"We will have to work on that this year. We will have to get you all baptized." They smiled in agreement.

"After this Jesus revealed himself again to the disciples by the Sea of Tiberias . . in this way. Some of them were together and Peter said, 'I am going fishing.'. . . Just as day was breaking, Jesus stood on the beach. . . . 'Children, have you any fish?' 'No,' they answered. He said to them, 'Cast the net on the right side of the boat, and you will find some.'

"On land, they saw a charcoal fire there, with fish lying on it, and bread. 'Come and have breakfast,' Jesus said" (John 21:1-12).

The moral of the story is this. Father Tom is not John the Baptist. André is not Andrew, and Carven is not Andrew's brother Simon. And Allen and Tony are not Nathanael and Philip. I am not Jesus. Lake Papakeechie is not the Sea of Galilee. And grilled hamburgers are not grilled fish.

But I suspect this is the way Jesus wants us to go about evangelizing. It was his style. I will say this much. The day all this happened was one of the best days I have had since I left Chicago, and it all happened on the Vigil of Pentecost. The Spirit of Jesus was hovering over Lake Papakeechie this day.

Friends for Different Seasons

IT is now springtime at Lake Papakeechie, and time to enjoy the changing seasons lakeside. The trees are in full foliage now, and summertime is bursting upon Heartland Indiana's lakes. Rowboats quietly pass my cottage as ice fishing gives way to casting. Sunset grows fuller each evening, and winter (and Lent) are over. We are in the afterglow of Pentecost.

I am struck by the renewal of friendships this time of year, when my lake friends come out of the long winter's solitude. We go through the winter without contact, but now our small lake community is alive again. It is time for spring cleaning, painting, gardening, berry-picking, and canning. It is strawberry and blueberry time, with fresh asparagus too.

We need to have friends for different seasons of our life, as well.

This summer our high school graduation class of 1941 will celebrate another reunion. Again, I am fortunate that many of my classmates live in the Fort Wayne area. It is a different kind of friendship than the one we shared forty-five years ago. We don't run together as we did as teenagers. Classmates have gone their respective professional and family ways. Most of them are grandparents these days.

But the memories of those carefree days together still bind us, and we have plenty to talk about and share. It is a wonderful experience to be a priest among all these friends from the past. As an observer of the passing scene, I see how we develop new friends at different stages of our lives. We seem to accumulate friends, but time and distance often separate us from earlier friendships.

Friendships will always exist in varying degrees of intensity and according to our situation in life.

We usually can number friends from high school and college days; for me, priestly friends from seminary days as well; friends from work, neighbors made in the parish or the community where we raise our families, even market friendships. (The English political philosopher Thomas Hobbes reduced all friendships to market friendships.)

Despite the fact that most of us can number countless different friendships as we grow older, in the end we usually settle down to a handful of really close, intimate friends. I pity anyone who does not have at least one close friend: a kind of crony, so to speak, who knows us as we really are, with all our foibles and weaknesses, but still enjoys our companionship.

I was reminded of this recently when I spent an evening with the retired bishop of Fort Wayne-South Bend, Bishop William McManus, who now lives in Chicago. The seven years we spent together under the same roof in Fort Wayne before his retirement were the stuff of just such a friendship. We could tolerate each other's foibles, share our failures and successes in a spirited, humor-filled exchange.

I suspect bishops, elected officials, public figures — presidents, kings, queens, all those who are in power and public view — often are isolated and stonewalled by their own closest advisors. Above all, such persons need a crony, a sidekick with whom they can let down their hair and be themselves in complete security.

We all need this, but especially public figures (like priests) who must play a role that is not our true selves. It is difficult to appear vulnerable and exposed, to admit to loneliness and isolation. Too often our publics are scandalized when they discover we might be human.

What I am saying is that friendships are absolutely essential to a balanced mental and spiritual life, but especially each of us needs one or two special friends who know us intimately and are not afraid to provide a balance wheel to our lives.

Thanksgiving

IT is getting deep into November, the month of witches, pumpkins, falling leaves, and the sounds of winter winds, the month of All Souls, the month of the dead, as Indian summer all of a sudden disappears and the trees become starkly bare. Winter is not far away.

I find myself this spooky night in the full blast of nature's stirring, vulnerable to all her mysterious ways. I am in my lakeside retreat cottage on Lake Papakeechie, where the four seasons come and go, coloring or discoloring my views.

I must tell you again about "the holy space," because around Labor Day I moved to an even more secluded place on the lake, this time down on the promontory point, at its very tip, where I have full view of the lake from both sides and where there is hardly anything stirring but Mother Nature herself.

For a year and a half, this lonely spot had been abandoned by the previous owner, when a death separated the retired couple who had lived here. In the absence of people, nature and wildlife moved in and took possession.

I have had a difficult time recapturing the idyllic setting from the raccoons, the Canadian honkers, the ducks, the chipmunks, and birds of all species who had in a way protected the place until God provided it for me to become their confidant. And so it has happened.

But this night the wind is howling, and I have never felt so alone in this isolated place, alone but supremely at ease with myself and with my Lord. All during my recent trip to Africa, when the going got toughest, I dreamed of Lake Papakeechie and yearned to return here to catch the last colors of Indian summer, never more beautiful in the Midwest and Indiana.

Catch them I did, barely, but enough to give me the leisure to write my articles on Ghana and Ethiopia. I thank God for the place he has provided me where I can put all these overseas visits to the trouble spots of the world into perspective.

There has been a kind of ebb and flow to my life the past several years. There have been the intense experiences on assignment to the trouble spots, such as Cambodia and Laos, Central America, Poland, Lebanon, and Africa, where people suffer much hardship and political turmoil. Then the return to Northern Indiana, where there is tranquillity, four seasons, fresh air and water, and abundant crops.

I say this in spite of unemployment, our own drought and shortfalls of crops, inflation, terrible recession, where many of our people have suffered deeply, especially minority groups.

But the malnutrition, the famine and drought, the contaminated water, the stunted growth and rampant diseases among children, high infant mortality rates, civil war, military coup after military coup and revolution, are an overwhelming experience for Third World people almost beyond the imagination of our affluent American society.

What has driven us to make these trips into the midst of God's poorest? Why did we seek out especially the refugee camps, the uprooted who have had to flee home and country after suffering famine, persecution, oppression, war, and random killing? We have been driven to do this in order to bring you their tragic stories, ugly and distasteful as they are, because we know your deep faith — that you would want to know where our sisters and brothers in Christ are suffering, and you would want to respond in your own way by prayer, sacrifice, and almsgiving. That is what Christ's universal Church is all about as we help carry one another's burdens.

These are the thoughts of Thanksgiving that whistle with the winds through my mind this lonely night at Lake Papakeechie. I thank God for bringing me safely home with the message, and for you who receive it.

Grandpa Bud

BLANCHE walked down the hill the other day to talk to me, as she is wont to do. Her husband, John (Bud), died last week at age seventy-nine of Alzheimer's disease. He had hoped to make it to eighty, as his father before him had.

Blanche had been faithfully at his bedside until the end, although he no longer recognized her or anyone, and had to be fed like an infant. "It was a blessing he died," she said, this thin but rugged woman whose features had been hewn from long life on a farm and staying outdoors in all kinds of weather.

Blanche reminds me a lot of my Aunt Rose of happy memory, who spent ninety-some years on the farm, taking care of family business, before she retired to a nursing home and then quietly died. These were strong women.

Blanche is my neighbor on Lake Papakeechie. She lives now alone, in a log house atop the hill. I live at the bottom in a small white cottage once owned by Blanche's brother and sister-in-law — until he died and she sold out. It was eighteen years ago that Blanche and Bud sold their farm and retired on Lake Papakeechie.

Bud loved to fish and mow that hill. "He had ten good years here, then Alzheimer's set in," Blanche said. The last eight years hadn't been easy for her as she stayed by his side at the nursing home some forty miles away.

But Blanche hung on at the cottage. That's her home. Only

recently has she been able to spend more time there because "there wasn't much I could do for Bud." Bud died peacefully, she said. "He looked so nice in the coffin."

Blanche will be spending her time at the lake now. "I love to be outdoors." She doesn't mind the winters. She takes care of her yard and her flowers — and there are lots of those.

But most of all, she takes care of her ducks and geese and other birds. They beat a steady path to her door, as predictable as a clock in their comings and goings. She feeds them and looks after them in the winter.

Just last week she told me about two ducks who come regularly every day. I often see them and can set my watch by them as they strut cautiously, looking right and left of the hill, past my deck to Blanche's house.

Then there was the wounded goose who got stuck in the snow last winter and couldn't fly because of a pulled wing. Once Blanche got him free, she nursed him for a few weeks until he was ready to fly again. One day he took off carefully and somewhat reluctantly. But he still comes to visit Blanche.

Blanche gets a lot of weekend help from her grandchildren, many of whom are now married but still remember as children coming to Lake Papakeechie and fishing with "Grandpa Bud." Those were great days they still recall, and how they remember Grandpa! Blanche is still here to receive them — and the next generation.

I am happy the good Lord took John in the spring. Blanche is now enjoying the spring and the summer days and has put her heart at rest. Someday she may sell this lovely place, but as she says, "not until someone wants it more than I do. They will have to pay a pretty price for it."

It is my favorite time of year — yard work and spring cleaning. Come June and July, a lot of fellowship will be celebrated here. Life will go on for all of us, yes, even for Blanche. Her critters will see to that. She won't be hurting for someone to take care of.

The Boys of Summer

I recently learned that Margaret Mead, the internationally known American anthropologist (1901-1978), wrote many of her classic works at a cottage on Lake Papakeechie not far from my little cottage. I can look across the corner of the lake and see her cottage as I sit on my deck and write this reflection.

The date is July 3, 1988. The place is drought-stricken Lake Papakeechie, where the water levels are low and the weeds are high. Not a good season for fishing. It is not quite as pleasant a view as Margaret Mead enjoyed years ago, but neither is drought-stricken Northern Indiana in this parched summer of 1988.

What do Margaret Mead and Sparky Anderson have in common this summer of 1988? Margaret Mead traveled the islands of the Pacific to study how culture influences personality. Sparky Anderson, famed manager of the Detroit Tigers, travels the American baseball- league cities to study the tribal culture of baseball teams.

The difference between Margaret Mead and Sparky Anderson is that Sparky plays out his anthropology 162 games a year. Margaret wrote about her findings. Margaret got to enjoy Lake Papakeechie. Sparky lives in locker rooms.

Those of you who know me know that I am a rabid Tiger fan, and an on-again, off-again Sparky Anderson fan. This season I am in Sparky's corner, and he has his charges in first place in the American League East as of July 3.

How does he do it? He is an anthropologist. He knows baseball players. He studies them. He has the ability to see in players something other managers can't see. He has the eyes of Margaret Mead.

How can a team that lost, through a system of free agency, a Lance Parish and Kirk Gibson in two years still be in first place midway through the season? Some say Sparky does it with mirrors. Others say he has gathered together a team of overachievers and over-the-hill players. Some say he does it with prayer (he is a Catholic) or by voodoo à la Margaret Mead.

I say Sparky is an anthropologist. He is a student of men and how to get the most out of them.

When the Tigers started the season with the likes of Pat Sheridan (overachiever), Larry Herndon (over-the-hill), Dave Bergman (not even a decent utility man last year), a washed-up Ray Knight, a retread by the name of Luis Salazar, and Tom Brookens (overachiever) — to mention a few — most people picked the Tigers for fifth place.

Guess who are hitting close to .300? Sheridan, Bergman, and Brookens. Herndon and Knight are hanging tough. Every night someone else picks up the team — Trammell (a cleanup hitter), Pettis (a no-hit speedster), or Lou Whitaker (his usual .280).

Who are these guys? Where did Sparky find them? How does he make winners out of losers? Ask Margaret Mead. If she were living today, she would be following the Detroit Tigers around the country. Forget the Pacific islands.

Then she and I could sit along the lakeshore of Papakeechie and discuss anthropology as it ought to be discussed in July, in baseball terms.

And I would tell her Sparky's secret — the age-old secret of winning baseball games. Good pitching and good defense have nothing to do with tribal customs.

Death Before Dawn

RALPH A. App, Lake Papakeechie, died early Thursday morning in his home.

With little variation, except for name and place, the above obituary appears every day in almost every newspaper in cities large and small. Very few of us fail to scan the obit pages of our newspapers each day to see if anyone we might have known has died.

Behind this and so many of the obits we read each day is a human story of heartbreak. You see, Ralph, age fifty-three, died unexpectedly. His wife, Dawn, found him dead in a chair in the morning from a massive heart attack. And as is the case in so many of these stories, there was no advance warning. In a twitch of an eyebrow, Ralph was dead and his wife of thirty-three years was left a widow.

Dawn's and Ralph's three lovely married daughters were left without their husband and father, and nine grandchildren were left without their grandfather. What this story is all about is sudden death that comes like a thief in the night, with no advance warning, and a family shattered by that death. It may be a heart attack, as is so often the case; it may be an accident, or whatever, but sudden death, unexpected death, is as much a reality in life as terminal diseases or deaths with dignity.

There is so much written today about death and dignity, how to handle the slow deaths of the terminally ill, or how to deal with "rational suicide," as it is called by some. People today spend a lot of time making pacts, drawing up living wills, or preparing instructions for their family in the event of death at the end of a long illness: what to do in event there is no longer rational communication, or when to "pull the plug."

But every so often we are faced with the unexpected death of a loved one, as Dawn App was this morning. "You must help me, Father Giese," is all she said when she called me. "I am going to need all the support I can get."

What do we say to someone in such a situation, when in the blink of an eye her whole life is shattered and turned upside down? What is the answer of faith we can give at such a moment?

At a time like this our theology books are not much help. Sure, we have the theology worked out. We have our resurrection theology to draw upon, all the promises of the risen Christ that he is preparing a final home for us, the rich theology of the risen Christ who suffered, died, and rose again so that we might share in his death and resurrection one day, so that we might live again one day for eternity.

The theology is helpful; the liturgy of the Mass of Resurrection, with its emphasis on celebration and hope, is helpful. Everything is put in perspective, but the emptiness, the grief, the trauma of a sudden death, whether spouse, child, or close friend, is still there, and after the funeral, all of this sets in.

The dead friend has gone to eternal happiness — this is our faith — but we who survive are back in reality of time and space and broken relationships. The time for our healing is at hand. It is at this point that our faith, not so much our theology, must sustain us.

Now Dawn is home alone for the first time. The house is the same, but her husband of thirty-three years is gone. The loneliness, grief, and emptiness set in for the first time. The reality that Ralph is gone for good sinks in. What to do? How to begin life anew? Where to start? Where is the hope for a better tomorrow? How to fill the void? What will it be like five or ten or fifteen years from now?

Since I knew that many of my readers have undergone this experience of emptiness and loneliness brought about by the unexpected death of a loved one, I called upon them to come to the aid of Dawn. I asked them to write a letter to Dawn and send it to me. I wanted them to offer some consolation to Dawn, to extend a helping hand, to share their experiences with sudden death, and to share how their faith sustained them, how they were able to cope in unexpected ways, how God graced them with a new and unexpected life.

Well, within a few weeks I had received over a hundred fifty "Letters to Dawn."

"The touch of another widow's hand says that I understand the grief that lingers on, the exclusion from the 'couples only' parties, the pain of holidays and anniversaries no longer shared." These words from just one letter I received last week.

How do we cope with unexpected death? The response has been overwhelming. What a beautiful thing to see good people healing one another, in a far more effective way that we professional ministers could do.

What impressed me in reading your letters was the time and effort you took to write a letter to Dawn, the love and concern you extended to one whom you've never met but shared something with in a deep way along life's journey.

A thought that came through so often was expressed by one person who said simply, "It has helped me trying to help Dawn. Putting my own experience and grief into words seemed to lighten my own burden."

You talked how important daily Mass, prayer, and the sacraments have been to you in times of grief. You urged Dawn to get involved in Church and community work, spend time with her children and grandchildren, write down her thoughts, and, above all, not be afraid to cry.

As one of you expressed it so well, "there is no formula for coping. Grief turns into fond memories."

There was heartbreak in your letter, too, as some of you talked about the loneliness that comes from separation caused by divorce, or separation, from infidelity in marriage, from alcoholism.

You spoke not only of the sudden death of a husband or wife, but also of parents, brothers, and sisters, young sons or daughters; not only from heart attacks but also from car accidents. So much Christian wisdom from "understanding hearts."

Dawn and her family have read, shared, and cried over your letters. You have brought her many healing graces. I would close this episode about Dawn with the other half of the quote I cited. "The touch of God's hand says I understand and I will sustain you through it all."

Jesus Came to Dinner

IT was Saturday evening on Lake Papakeechie. I had invited Helen and Chesty Snedler and Dawn App over for a deck party. Chesty is a retired Lutheran pastor now living on Papakeechie, after thirty-five years of pastoring in Willoughby, Ohio. We have become very close friends.

Dawn is still living year-round at Papakeechie and enjoying her grandchildren. The winters get long. She has developed her own interior decorating service and has redone her own lake home by herself.

On Saturday morning Dawn and Loretta, a friend of mine from Chicago, went blueberry picking at Wolf Lake. Loretta has been spending several weeks with me at Lake Papakeechie. She has been tidying up the cottage and helping me entertain my wonderful neighbors.

When Helen, Chesty, and Dawn arrived Saturday evening, our deck party was threatened by a heavy but soft rainfall. But then the much-needed rain stopped and a beautiful haze fell over the lake, and we could see a bright sunset streaming through it. The lake became like a mirror, parted only by a flock of baby geese with their mother floating across the water, followed by some baby ducks who came ashore to eat. It became a quiet, still evening.

About that time Jesus and his apostles came by unexpectedly to join us. Jesus had been preaching over on the Wawasee side of the lake. His apostles had just returned from their first mission. Jesus had sent them out two-by-two earlier in the area of Goshen, Indiana. He had instructed them to take nothing with them on the journey but a walking stick — no food, no traveling bag, no money. They were out preaching repentance, expelling demons, and anointing the sick.

They had just returned and were eager to tell Jesus what they had done and what they had taught. Jesus suggested they get into a boat and go where they could rest a bit. They pushed off and rowed across to our place, where we were joined by Martha and Mary. Jesus told Peter to catch a few fish off my dock, where we have a lot of paddies and it is generally good fishing. Helen made a few loaves of her famous sourdough bread, and I had a nice bottle of red wine.

It was a joyful party with Jesus and the apostles, only to be interrupted a little bit later when the lake people found out Jesus was there and came to see him. What we didn't know at the time, and I doubt Jesus told his apostles — we were going to need those loaves of sourdough bread and those fishes Peter caught to feed a hungry group of people. Some estimated five hundred had come down the promontory point, where I live, to hear Jesus preach. Jesus just took the loaves and fishes, gave thanks, and passed them around to all those people.

The next Sunday I told the parishioners about this at St. Martin de Porres parish in Syracuse, where I was helping out.

Dawn and Loretta put up quite a bit of blueberry preserves this week. We just never know when Jesus and the young men will be dropping by. I know, I'll never have another deck party without Jesus being invited. And I won't worry about running out of wine!

Unscheduled Prayer

J ESUS seemed in a grumpy mood, as Mark relates the story (11:13 ff.). First, he cursed the fig tree because it was barren at a time when he was hungry for its fruit. Then he chased the moneychangers out of the temple in a rare display of anger. Now it was the next day as he and the apostles were on the road again when they passed by the fig tree Jesus had cursed. To the dismay of the apostles, it had withered and died.

It was at about this point that Jesus taught his apostles how to pray. "Put your trust in the Lord. I solemnly assure you, whoever says to this mountain, 'Be lifted up and thrown into the sea,' and has no doubts but believes that what he says will happen, shall have it done to him.

"I give you my word, if you are ready to believe that you will receive whatever you ask for in prayer, it shall be done for you. When you stand to pray, forgive anyone against whom you have a grievance so that your heavenly Father may in turn forgive you your faults."

It was New Year's Eve and I had just taken four of the guys to Lake Papakeechie for a few days of vacation. About 10:30 in the evening they asked me if we could pray together. And so we took the Scripture readings for the New Year's Day Mass and read them together. André's favorite prayer is the Apostles' Creed, so he led us in praying it.

The guys played cards until midnight, then we ushered in the New Year. At 1:30 André suggested we celebrate Mass rather than in the morning. So we celebrated a very intimate Mass together around the dining room table. Then they played cards the rest of the night, and I went to bed.

Unscheduled and spontaneous prayer meetings with these young apostles are not isolated. They happen often when we are together, always accompanied by Scripture reading, followed by prayer. I am continually amazed at the naturalness, spontaneity, and simplicity of their prayer life, and edified by it. The boys are teaching me to pray as well.

In the evening we were reviewing together for a high school religion test they had coming up, and the subject matter was the sacraments. This night, it was on baptism, but then I jumped ahead a bit and began talking about the Sacrament of Penance and Rite of Reconciliation. After the review, the boys wanted to pray together, so we had our customary prayer session. When it was completed, one of the guys asked to go to confession. It turned out to be a beautiful evening, not at all what I expected.

I am looking forward now to organizing a special Sunday liturgy for these kids and their friends — perhaps on a monthly basis to begin with, then perhaps weekly. It would be a kind of Base Christian Community, but where we could gather together for prayer and worship, for tutoring, jobs and academic counseling, for breaking bread together. Jesus said, "Have you not read this scripture: / 'The very stone which the builders rejected / has become the head of the corner;/ this was the Lord's doing, and it is marvelous in our eyes'?" (Mark 12:10-11).

It looks as if we are going to learn how to pray together, as Jesus taught his disciples. It looks as if we are going to need a kind of upper room where we can break bread together, as Jesus did the night before he died. "The Teacher says, 'Where is my guest room where I am to eat the passover with my disciples?'. . . And as they were eating, he took bread, and blessed, and broke it, and gave it to them, and said, 'Take; this is my body.'"

Maybe the little cottage at Lake Papakeechie is the upper room.

Growing Up in Indiana

IT is that time of year again on Lake Papakeechie. As August nears, we begin our trek into the countryside in search of the bountiful fruits and vegetables and wildflowers our good God has provided for us in this beginning of harvest time.

The fields are green with corn and soybeans, and the smell of new-mown hay excites our nostrils. It is the time for tender sweet corn, Michigan peaches, home-grown tomatoes, sweet melons, and a bounty of flowers and greens. It is the time when we seek out the farmers' markets for fresh produce — if we haven't already grown it in our own backyards and truck patches.

When I was a boy growing up on a farm in northern Indiana, the summer evening suppers my mother prepared with fried spring chicken, sweet corn, ripe beefsteak tomatoes, hot buttered beets, and green beans and ham hocks, all of it grown on our small farm, were an absolute delight. It was the time of year we all looked forward to, and as though not to lose it, my mother was busy canning peaches, tomatoes, beans, corn, and pickled beets for the long winter months.

But it never came easy on the farm. Before the harvest there were those anxious moments over whether or not the rains would come, followed by the hot growing sunshine. Perhaps no one is more conscious of the elements and the need to rely so completely on a provident God than farm folk. Because of their dependency on God, farmers have a deep faith and a profound sense of gratitude for the goodness of God.

Before the harvest, before the first fruits could be offered back to God, there were the long hours in the fields preparing the soil, cultivating, weeding — and praying. It began in the early spring and continued through the hot summer months into the early fall.

How well I recall those hot summer days when my father would gather up his three sons to go into the fields to hoe those dreaded Canada thistles. It was then I learned my father's concern for the good seed, that it not get entangled by thistles and thorns. It was then that I would take a leisurely Sunday evening walk with him through all the fields to see how each crop was growing and what crop would need special attention come Monday morning.

It was a slow, laborious process to bring all this to fruition come late July and early August, but when the harvest came, we could look back upon it all, as God himself did when he created the world, then pronounce it "Good."

Even the Scriptures this time of year speak to us about planting and harvesting. When preaching among the Palestinian farmers in his day, Jesus himself talked about the good seed and the bad seed falling on hard ground and among thorns, and about the birds feeding on it before it could take root.

Over and over he and the prophets before him tell us how the seed is the Word of God, how some of it falls on good ground and produces thirty-fold, but some of it never takes root and dies.

The Scriptures sing of the soft rains and snow, sent gratuitously by God to prepare the bed for the seed to take root, and how the Word of God also comes like a gentle rain, not to disappear into the earth but to come back to God a hundredfold. Sometimes we accept the Word of God, but often enough we let it fall on the hardened ground, where it dies.

This is the time of year we should get out into the country to see the verdant fields, pick wildflowers, sit by a lakeside, enjoy a brilliant sunset, and saturate ourselves with the beauties of God's handiwork. It will renew our faith and reinvigorate our stressful lives.

It is the time of year when everything is open to everyone. Even the poor can break the dreariness of their lives and enjoy the fresh fruits and vegetables much cheaper than other times of the year — not the hothouse variety we live on many months of the year. It is healthy time for the rich and the poor alike.

When I spent twelve years as a priest in the inner city of Chicago, I missed much of this. Not that farmers' markets were not available — even the large cities are setting them up in the downtown areas — but the poor people, locked in high-rise tenements, never smelled the flowers or saw the verdant countryside. Summers are hot and drab in the asphalt jungles of America, where hardly a tree or even grass can be seen, let alone fields ripe with produce.

To be denied contact with the beauty of God's creation may be the greatest social sin of all. To enjoy it seems to me the greatest human right of all.

Life on the Farm

THE bitter cold which settled in on the midwest brings back memories, I am sure, of past winters. I can remember winters when it is was cold upstairs in our farmhouse. The only heat was what came through a vent in the ceiling of the kitchen-dining room downstairs, where a coal-burning stove heated those two rooms.

Most of our life was spent in the kitchen and dining area. The parlor, reserved for times when guests visited, was closed off in the wintertime.

On Saturday nights, we took our baths in the kitchen in a large washtub filled with heated water. Until I was a sophomore in high school, we read and studied by kerosene lamps — only later did rural electrification come through.

Without electricity, we still had to pump our water from a well outside, and of course the trip to the outhouse in the wintertime, when we had to brush the snow off the two-seater, was a dreaded experience.

As school-aged kids, we had to brave the cold outdoors to do chores — feeding the chickens and pigs, milking the cows — each morning long before sunrise. We carried our lanterns to the barn, along with a bucket of hot water to wash the cow's teats before beginning our milking by hand.

Getting up early in those cold bedrooms upstairs — rushing downstairs to dress by the stove, which by now had very little heat left in it, then out into the cold morning air — was no Fourth of July picnic. By the time the chores were finished, and we came back into the house, the smell of bacon and eggs and freshly perked coffee greeted us. The kitchen was aglow with warmth — for a few precious moments until it was time to leave again for school. Then, it was a ten-mile trip into Fort Wayne to Central Catholic High School.

In the evenings, we had to go through the routine all over again — the chores, dinner, family Rosary, the homework by kerosene lamps. Needless to say, we went to bed early. And so the days and nights passed in the wintertime.

I recall how I envied my classmates in Fort Wayne, who rolled out of bed in heated homes, caught a city bus to school, and never experienced the hardships of life on a farm during wintertime. We had moved to the farm from Fort Wayne in the heart of the depression. As a grammar-school pupil, I had been spoiled by all the conveniences of city life: inside plumbing, electricity, no chores to do early in the morning or later at night.

My father, at age forty-nine, fed up with the depression and life in the city, decided to go back to farming. He scraped up enough money to buy eighty acres, two horses, a cow, and a used Fordson tractor. So back to the farm we went — Dad, Mom, and the three boys. It was hard on my mother at first, but in time we got electricity, a telephone, and a three-lane highway past our farmhouse. Life improved.

On Sunday afternoons during those long winter months, our pastor would come over, and we would spend the afternoon playing euchre or pinochle. Our pastor loved those sessions, but once spring and summer came, we changed to croquet in our front yard. Our pastor was a stickler on the rules — the way he played at the seminary in Baltimore — and we were forever having arguments.

Our pastor, in his early fifties, was a convert and a very cultured man. I recall as a college student walking up and down the grounds of our country parish, as he read Father John Bannister Tabb's poetry to me. He would persist until I went to the convent to con the good Sisters out of a bottle of altar wine, so we could mix our poetry with wine.

During the hot summer months, when we were in the fields making hay or threshing, he would often join in the work awhile, then go into town for a keg of beer to treat the men at the end of a hot day.

Our pastor, a good man, very involved with young people in the parish, gave us religious instructions once a week, promoted the CYO, and was interested in the rural life of the area. He lived alone in a big, old country rectory, doing his own cooking and laundry. I learned a lot from him that has stood me in good stead as a priest.

Remembering Father

IF my Dad were alive today, he would be over the hundred-year mark, not an unusual age for some of his family members. One sister lived to be ninety-eight, another in her nineties was still active as a Sister of Saint Francis in Joliet, Illinois, until her death. My father died young, age sixty-three, of cancer. At the time I was thirty years old and working in Chicago. It was long before I had decided to become a priest, and so neither of my parents were living when I entered the seminary, later to be ordained. I am sure they would have approved.

Both of my parents came from solid Catholic farming families in Indiana. I recall as a youngster visiting the Giese homestead at Dunnington, Indiana. Dad was the leader of the Giese clan, the one the others came to for advice. He never had any education beyond grammar school. Back in those days it was four years downstairs and four years upstairs in the schoolhouse, with lots of time off to work in the fields. He was also a semi-pro baseball player who spent several summers in the minor leagues and eventually had his own baseball team in Dunnington called the Giese Goslins. That was about the time he and Mom got married. He spent years teaching me how to throw the roundhouse curve, the upshoot, and the downshoot.

After they got married, my folks settled in Fort Wayne, where my Dad took up the carpentry trade until the depression of the 1930s wiped him out. After a few years operating a horse-drawn milk wagon during the depression, he moved back to the farm. He was a good farmer, and during the winter months he kept up his carpenter's trade of building cabinets. The vestment cabinets in our little country church, St. Aloysius in Yoder, are still there to remind us of his handiwork.

We held on to the farm for seventeen years, and Dad became a community leader who spearheaded bringing rural electrification and the telephone into the area. He made a success of his eighty acres and lived in the country until he died.

Talking about death was something my father wanted to do once he found out he was dying of cancer. It was forty-three years ago last summer that he found out he had terminal cancer of the colon and was given a few months to live. A strong, strapping man, he was the picture of health when he got the news. He and another man had just built a barn during the hot summer months.

Immediately after the exploratory operation, the doctor called the family together and broke the news. We insisted he tell my father as soon as possible. He was a strong man, we said, and he could handle it. Besides, you couldn't hide it from him anyway. The doctor said he would find an appropriate moment to tell him.

The following Sunday when we came to visit him, he was in high spirits. But then he couldn't keep it locked up any longer, broke down, and told us the doctor had told him he had only a few months to live. Amid all our tears, he said he was happy to know. He had always prayed for advance notice, so that he could prepare properly for death. His prayers had been answered. He thanked God for this.

We were living on the farm at the time — long before Hospice, chemotherapy, and all the other modern technologies to deal with cancer. My father insisted on coming home to die. He didn't want to be all wired up in a cold, impersonal hospital room.

My father began immediately to make his plans. First of all, he got the farm in order, so my mother wouldn't have to worry about that. He got his bills paid, the taxes worked out, and announced a public auction at which the farm, all his farm equipment, tools, and cattle would be sold. That was a sad day for him as he saw people bidding on all he owned, then hauling it away — especially his carpentry tools.

He made all his own funeral plans. At the same time he began making his spiritual preparations. We lived a in a small rural parish. The forty-year-old priest came every morning to bring my father Communion and spend time with him praying and discussing death.

The last month all three of his sons went home to be with him and Mom until the end. It was perhaps the most powerful spiritual experience in my life to see this man deal with suffering and death. Each evening until almost the very end he insisted on leading the family Rosary, as he done all our lives after dinner.

Some nights he was bent double with pain, but he always completed the Rosary. We watched him grow weaker, lose weight, and in a real sense dispossess himself of everything — his material things, his tools, his farm, his health — to a point where he stood naked face-to-face with God. Each day he had to let go of something else.

Several days before he died, he gave me a list of men in the rural community and asked me to call them in. He wanted to see then one by one before he died. I remember when those ruddy farm men, most of them around his age, came to our farm and visited with my Dad for the last time. They emerged from his room in tears. Then I found out what it was all about.

These men, whom my Dad had been contacting as a member of the St. Vincent de Paul Society in our parish, had fallen away from the Church, and my Dad wanted one last go at them on his deathbed. One by one, he took them on. It was then I realized how much good my father had been doing in our little parish in a quiet way, and we knew nothing about it until he died. So many came up to us at his wake, complete strangers, to tell us of some small act of kindness he had done for them.

My father died peacefully with all of us, including the parish priest, at his bedside. We were praying with him when he died. He had gotten his house in order during that three-month period, and it was time to leave us. I can't remember a more beautiful death.

Those last three months of his life were perhaps the greatest legacy he left to his family. He made stronger persons out of us, and who knows? — but seven years later I entered the priesthood. I feel his presence yet today.

A Nostalgic Return

IT was a nostalgic return to my alma mater, St. Joseph's College, Rensselaer, Indiana, one June Saturday afternoon. We drove through the farmlands of Indiana along a route I often hitchhiked between Fort Wayne and St. Joe some fifty years ago. It was the same area, not far from the college, where Grandfather

Giese put down his roots and began farming, when he arrived at age nineteen from Münster, Westphalia, Germany.

When I attended St. Joe College, it was a small boys' school of five hundred students. It was just beginning to blossom as a four-year college. Early on, it had been a preparatory college seminary for priests studying for the Society of the Precious Blood.

In the year 1941, when I showed up as a seventeen-year-old farm boy from the Fort Wayne area, St. Joseph's College had its largest freshman class. Its football team was in the midst of a three-year undefeated streak. Its baseball team would produce the likes of Gil Hodges (a classmate), one of the Boys of Summer of the Brooklyn Dodgers, who was to die prematurely as manager of the New York Mets.

Room, board, tuition, and all expenses were five hundred dollars a year, as the German Precious Blood Community of Sisters prepared all the meals. We had lots of sauerkraut and mashed potatoes. Crops and cattle were homegrown on the college farms. Lay brothers worked the farms, which had the richest soil in Indiana.

Classes were small. Almost all of the professors were priests of the Precious Blood, and most of them from Mercer County, Ohio, which gave so many vocations to the community. Students could wander in an out of the professors' rooms day and night, if an inquisitive mind desired.

I thought I had died and gone to heaven in this rural setting not far from Chicago. I was the first member of the Giese clan ever to go to college. My folks were struggling with a small farm, as it was still the years of the Great Depression.

Thanks to a scholarship, I made my way to St. Joe and began work on the college publications. It was at St. Joseph's that a budding journalist was born.

Father Syl Ley, himself a product of Whitley county near Huntington, Indiana, became my mentor in journalism. Father Ley practiced what he taught. He was a superb journalism, English, and Latin teacher.

It wasn't long before I was involved with *Stuff*, the college newspaper, and *Measure*, the college literary journal. By the time of my junior year I was editing both, and in my senior year Father Ley had me working in the Public Information Office and editing the alumni paper, *Contact*.

Pearl Harbor was attacked in December 1941. Within two years the college began to empty out. Enrollment fell to one sixty, but the college survived and came back strong after the war. Fortunately, because of a physical problem, I missed the draft and stayed on at the college, where I graduated in 1945.

St. Joe College was where it all began. Those were the happiest days of my life.

St. Joseph's College remains a wonderful Catholic Liberal Arts College, with enrollment well over a thousand. Its widely acclaimed Core Program remains close to Newman's Idea of a University.

The Dreams of Boyhood Fulfilled

IT was cramped and filled with cigarette smoke, but for a few hours during this chilly, windswept afternoon in northern Indiana, it was shelter. More than that, for a few hours I fulfilled a dream of my youth. There aren't many more boyhood dreams for me to realize, except perhaps to sit someday on the bench with the Detroit Tigers during a major-league baseball game.

The occasion this Saturday afternoon in Indiana was the St. Joseph's College-Butler University football game. It was not all that inspiring, as my alma mater, St. Joe, went down to a 31-16 defeat, despite some excellent passing from a kid named Fazio.

What is it that makes those Italian-American kids such excellent quarterbacks? Another fellow named Fazio, the coach of the Pittsburgh Panthers, was going down to defeat the same afternoon, and by the same score, at the hands of Notre Dame (also my alma mater), and a kid named Marino pitched his heart out for Pittsburgh but lost.

I hadn't been back to St. Joe college for some years and hadn't seen a football game since my student years — 1941-45 —

those years when World War II broke out and our peak college enrollment of five hundred quickly reduced to a hundred sixty until after the war.

The years 1940-41 were great football years at St. Joe College, as the Pumas were undefeated under the driving force of Joe Dienhart, later to join Purdue's coaching staff. St. Joe College was loaded with rough and tough street kids from Chicago and Northern Indiana. The monsters of Rensselaer in those years were the likes of Sunagel, Gilpin, the Scollards, Lapsys, Ellspermann, Wisniewski — and no less than Gil Hodges, who later became a baseball hero in Brooklyn and manager of the New York Mets.

Gil played baseball, basketball, and football at St. Joe, and it is hard to say which was his best sport.

In those days, as an aspiring journalist, I did sportswriting for the St. Joe weekly paper, *Stuff*, mostly by running up and down the field with pen and pad. I had great aspirations of becoming a sportswriter for one of the Chicago dailies.

As you can see, it never happened. The Lord had other outlets planned for my journalistic skills. So you can imagine the palpitation in my heart when Father Charles Banet, C.PP.S., St. Joe's energetic president, invited me to sit in the press box to enjoy the game.

Our booth had about five young radio broadcasters from college radio, including color commentators. I could relate to their emotional play-by-play coverage. It took me back some forty years to a young sports reporter and the joys of writing up a game for the campus newspaper. That's how journalistic careers are born.

When I had squinted my eyes and let my mind drift back in time, I could see George Ellspermann and Gil Hodges cutting through the weak side of the line for big gains, Tom Scollard catching passes, Gilpin and Sunagel opening the holes. It all came from my vantage point in the press box.

Those were some of happiest days of my life. After the game I caught up with a few professors from those earlier days, now ancient Fathers and Brothers. They were giants in my day, some forty years ago, and still are my scholastic heroes today.

Second Fiddle

A NEWS photo published recently, showing a man being reunited with his violin after it had been stolen and then recovered, revealed an expression of indescribable joy, and I could understand why.

A man's violin is as sacred as his wife, and for anyone to play another person's violin amounts to infidelity. Over the years a relationship between a person and his violin develops into the closest encounter. Of all friends a person may have, none may ever be closer than his violin; certainly none will be more responsive to his every mood and emotion, always responding, neither more nor less but always in perfect empathy with its master. The second great commandment could have read: "And to love your neighbor as you love your violin." A violin is an alter ego.

When I was very young, perhaps seven, a family violin was handed down to me. Why to me, I'll never know, except somehow I picked out "Twinkle, Twinkle, Little Star" the first time I held it in my arms. Having neither an ear for music nor those long slender fingers so essential, I was a most unlikely one to master the intricacies of the violin. Alas, it was my destiny, and years later as an aspiring journalism student in college, I penned an essay entitled "Second Fiddle" as a kind of autobiographical piece. It still holds.

During grammar school, I was a little tyke, not much taller than my old wooden violin case was long. We were an ungainly sight in the neighborhood of Fort Wayne, Indiana, where my fiddle case and I grew up together. Though I might stop to play ball, leaving it behind, using it as a storehouse for all the things a boy carries with him from lunch to books — and, of course, the violin — we were inseparable.

High school didn't offer much of an improvement — my mother was a persistent woman. I played second fiddle in the Central Catholic High School orchestra. Even on graduation night, I dressed not in cap and gown but in silk cape and white pants and shirt and spent the evening in the orchestra pit playing second fiddle. It was the pits.

The violin became a fiddle when we moved to the farm near Yoder, Indiana, during my high school years, as some feeble attempts were made to play the fiddle at parish square dances and, of course, always to play "Silent Night" solo at Midnight Mass. Then on to college we went to begin life anew, this time in the St. Joe College orchestra, under the baton of the unforgettable Prof Tonner, movable wig and all, who corralled me in the college orchestra, with free lessons thrown in, not that they would ever help me.

When I decided to abandon the orchestra in my sophomore year to engage in more cultural pursuits, such as the Poetry Society and the school newspaper, Prof Tonner was indignant. One morning he came knocking at my door to reenlist me in the orchestra — simply because that new batch of seminarians from Brunnerdale played less than invigorating second fiddle. Professor Tonner missed my zest and enthusiasm. To me a second fiddle was a second fiddle, but for him there was a difference, so back I went for another year.

When life led me to Chicago, we had a small family combo, as we did some home jazz improvisations and played and sang folk music. It was good fun. But in 1962, at the tender age of thirty-seven, I began my belated seminary studies in Rome. The violin was left behind in an attic in Chicago, where it gathered dust. When I embraced the celibate life, I put my mistress away. No more fiddling around.

Yet, I must confess to one last fling, in 1963, in Vienna, Austria, where I spent a summer as a seminarian in an old Baroque church where Haydn himself once played and prayed. Vienna always breathes of music. One summer evening I visited some friends who had gathered a few people together in the kitchen as a kind of string quartet to make music for the pure joy of it.

They tucked a spare violin under my chin as we played *Die Fledermaus*. I haven't touched a violin since. That was a high enough note on which to stop. Nothing in life could ever match the ecstatic moment. *Die Fledermaus* in Vienna. Second fiddle at its best!

Twenty years had now passed since I played my violin in

Vienna, and I have given some thought, if only nostalgically, to taking it up again, arthritis permitting, in retirement.

In fact, it wasn't until then I was tempted at a dinner banquet to play again. I was handed another man's violin, but I couldn't bring myself to defile it. After so much shared experience with my own violin, I knew something of the intimacy that must have existed between him and his violin, such as I have enjoyed with mine. So many shared emotions, so many moments of joy and sorrow, so many ups and downs with the bow, and always the violin was there to respond, to talk back and somehow understand. I could never defile that man's violin. I could not enter that intimate relationship.

Besides, dear old Professor Tonner had said it all forty years ago at St. Joseph's College. "Giese, you can never play another violin but yours, and no one will ever be able to play yours but you." It was as though he were pronouncing marriage vows between my violin and me. For better or worse, we were destined to spend our lives together until death do us part.

You see, as a boy in Fort Wayne, banging that violin around in that oversized wooden box, I had broken it many times, only to take it to my grandfather to have it mended. He would saw a little off there, sand a little here, and glue it back together. Over the years, almost imperceptibly, except to Prof Tonner's exacting fingers, it had shrunk in size.

Prof Tonner was right. Only I could play it, stubby fingers and all, because I had grown up with it. The violin and I got used to each other's shortcomings, like a husband and a wife growing old together. I'd grown accustomed to its voice.

Well, after twenty minutes, which seemed like an hour, of storytelling and giving the history of my violin and how it became a fiddle when I became a country boy, I placed the violin gently back in its box and sat down. Those who were in attendance laughed and enjoyed my storytelling, but they were disappointed I never touched bow to strings.

I am consoled that I don't stand alone in my reverence for the fiddle. Venerable John Henry Newman once wrote a few words to a friend about his fiddle. I'll share them with you:

"I never wrote more than when I played the fiddle. I always sleep better after music. There must be some electric current passing from the strings through my finger into the brain and down the spinal marrow. Perhaps thought is music" (John Henry Newman, Letter to W. Church, June 11, 1865).

Gypsy Violin

IT will be forever my gypsy violin. I am on a Swiss airline flight from Warsaw to New York as I write this, after ten days of following Pope John Paul II on his pilgrimage to Poland.

I am carrying with me in a cloth bag a violin which I bought in a flea market in Warsaw for sixty dollars. And I am thrilled with my "refugee Polish violin." But first, let me tell you a story. You will recall my affair with the violin when I was growing up as a boy in Fort Wayne. I told you how I had abandoned my violin some twenty years ago, but hope one day to pick it up again. That is the background.

But now I was in Warsaw, where I learned about its famous flea market. Our guide took us there at the end of the papal visit. It was a fascinating experience. Thousands of people converged on the flea market, but not quite as many as followed the Holy Father.

It is a giant garage sale, with everything imaginable available from antiques to ancient coins to parts for hi-fi equipment, cars, or radios. I was single-minded, looking for a violin. I found three or four, but not quite what I wanted. Nor was the price right.

Then, an apparition! An elderly, wandering minstrel, a gypsy troubadour, strolled through the market with several violins in hand. We stopped. We negotiated. He wanted dollars. I had them. The price started at a hundred dollars. He came down to eighty. I offered fifty; we settled for sixty.

He played the violin for me. It sounded magnificent and in perfect tune. He inserted it in a cloth sack and I walked away with my "gypsy violin."

Somewhere in rural Indiana I will soon put violin to chin again, after so many years. Maybe the romance will be over.

Maybe my arthritic fingers will refuse my spirit. But somehow the gypsy violin has found a new home in a new, free world.

In my quiet moments the violin and I will cry again and sing again and express again what feeble emotion I can arouse — after so many years of absence from playing. My gypsy violin, my Polish refugee violin, will remind me ever anew of Pope John Paul's return to Poland. Like the Pontiff himself, the gypsy violin will sing of freedom, of human rights, of Solidarity. It will capture, as he did, the spirit of a free and independent Poland, groaning for new life and renewal.

Who knows the history of a nation better than a wandering gypsy violin — or a pilgrim pope? Wherever Pope John Paul traveled in Poland, he stirred the nationalistic and religious spirits of the people. He sang of Poland's days of victories and nights of defeat. He praised its saints and *beati* and linked them with the thousand-year history of Catholic Poland and six hundred years of the Black Madonna of Czestochowa.

A gypsy violin knows the history as well. How many provinces and festivals and bistros has my violin played in? How many times has it expressed the joys and sorrows of Poland? Only my imagination can supply the answers. But my Polish violin will now sing the songs of Poland to me and forever remind me of the hopes John Paul II released again in this beleaguered nation.

My gypsy violin knows the story of Poland. A French newsmagazine, *L'Exprés*, titles its issue, "*Jean Paul II, Roi de Pologne*. John Paul II, King of Poland." King of Eastern Europe — Poland, Czechoslovakia, Yugoslavia, Bulgaria, the newly liberated Soviet Union.

The gypsy violin knows the secret well. It has traveled the area. And now the whole world knows, because of a pilgrim pope.

Gullible Giese

I BECAME stuck with the name "Gullible Giese" years ago, as a student at St. Joseph's College in Indiana, when a group of classmates played a trick on me. As we walked across the campus each morning to class, they would stop and set their watches by the City Hall clock some two miles away. Only weeks later did I discover that they could no more see the tower clock — or even City Hall — than I could, but I believed them and attributed it to my poor vision. "Gullible Giese," they called me.

They had me right. Indeed I am gullible. Some fifty years later I am still perceived as being gullible. Maybe that is how I became a priest. Anyone can run a game on me. As recently as a few years ago, when I was hauling teenagers back and forth to school activities, a friend said to me that the kids could be smoking pot in the back of my station wagon and I wouldn't even know it. He may have been on the right track.

Kids can pull my leg, do a snow job on me, play games, and I still believe them. I am a sucker, an easy touch, too tender-hearted, naïve, simplistic, and trusting.

Trusting. Ah, that's the word. That's the secret of being gullible. It comes from being without guile, and therefore believing others I deal with are without guile. I leave myself open. I can be had. By some, that is considered a terrible weakness. It has cost me hundreds of dollars. I believe every hard-luck story. I reach in my pocket.

Only once has a man told me the truth, and even then I was gullible. He asked me for a dollar instead of twenty-five cents, because he wanted a drink, not a cup of coffee. No use in lying. "G.G." gave it to him.

Of course, at my age, I have rationalized my lifetime of being gullible. I have linked it with priesthood — even with celibacy. To be a priest is to be gullible. Not every seasoned, experienced pastor would agree with me. We tend to become more cynical as we become older. I tend to become even more gullible — more trusting and believing.

A small book, *The Celibacy Myth*, by Charles Gallagher and Thomas Vandenberg, two priests, offers their statement to priests who tend to get negative and down when life seems to be overcoming goodness:

"People are unreasonable, illogical, and self-centered. Love them anyway.

"If you do good, people will accuse you of selfish, ulterior motives. Do good anyway.

"If you are successful, you will make false friends and true enemies. Succeed anyway.

"The good you do will be forgotten tomorrow. Do good anyway.

Honesty and transparency make you vulnerable. Be honest and transparent anyway.

"What you spend years building may be destroyed overnight. Build anyway.

"People really need help but may attack you if you really help them. Help people anyway.

"Give the world the best you have and you will be kicked in the teeth. Give the world the best anyway.

"If you choose to live a life of communion with your people, making them the first priority in your life, you will be judged old-fashioned. Live with your people anyway.

"When you openly proclaim your love for your people, you will be dismissed as hopelessly idealistic. Proclaim your love anyway."

In other words, that's being gullible.

What is the dynamic of being gullible? I think it is the innate goodness of people, especially when measured against our own sinfulness. People come to priests because they need help — that's about the only time they come. Their needs range far and wide, age to age, but priests after all are ordained for people.

The story has been told of a famous American author who made his first visit to Ireland to give a prestigious lecture. When he was greeted at the airport, he was invited to make a substantial donation to a subscription drive. Indeed, he made a generous donation, but he opened his lecture with these words: "I came as a stranger and you 'took me in.' "

It is easy to prejudge, to doubt the sincerity of those who come to us for help, but it is difficult to walk in the shoes of another. What might be a major need for one could be an insignificant need for us — for example, a friend to talk to, a place to sleep, a bowl of soup, a Christmas basket, a handout, a greeting, a warm embrace, an encouraging word.

To put it simply, people do come to us, especially as priests, for help. Most often we meet each other like passing ships in the night. What should be the initial attitude? A closed door, a closed heart, a cynical rebuke, an empty hand, a referral, a reproach, a bodily gesture that says, "No, not you again"?

Gullibility means to accept people as they are. To hear their story, to make a one-on-one contact, to reflect the love of Jesus. To accept. To believe. To care. To help.

. Several years ago I met a young man on the streets of Chicago. He stopped me and asked, "Aren't you Father Giese?" I responded, yes. He said I wouldn't remember him — it had been nearly ten years, but he was the surly teenager who had caused all kinds of trouble at a weekly teen dance I had sponsored in the parish.

How could I forget? He gave me fits. He was rude, disruptive, foul-mouthed, arrogant, and on drugs. Many a night I had to close the dance early because of him. One hardhead could spoil it for everyone else.

This day, on the streets of Chicago ten years later, a clean-cut youth stops me to thank me for all I did for him, for tolerating him, and not giving up on him. Today, he said, he has worked through his problems. Life is going well with him. He just wanted to say, "Thank you."

We just never know. Facts indeed may prove us wrong on occasion, on afterthought. We may err. We may misjudge. We may regret. We may be hurt in the encounter. What we thought would bring new hope to a person may only prolong an inevitable end in misery and despair. We both may fall.

A turn down a new path in life may never happen for the one we trust. Or the person (I am thinking of young people now) may find a new direction in life because someone believed in him or her at a point of life when everyone else did not.

We will never know what grace of God brought us together — sometimes for a brief, passing encounter, sometimes for the beginning of a long-lasting relationship. Some have estimated that it really takes five full years to develop a lasting friendship.

What I am saying is this: Be gullible. Be open. Don't close your heart. Don't prejudge. Let the grace of God work. We will never know, nor need to know, the effects of a gesture of love, even if the other person believed at the moment that he or she had "taken us in." Err on the side of the angels.

The late beloved Pope John XXIII's advice for governing the Church also applies for relationships. "Observe everything. Keep a blind eye to most of it. Correct very little."

What is the relationship of gullibility and gratitude. The more gullible we are, the less gratitude we should expect. Gullibility is really not concerned with gratitude.

When working with young people, I often hear from some cynical adults that the young people will not be grateful. "Are you appreciated for what you are doing for them? Do they ever say, 'Thank you'?" what is gratitude and what is appreciation? No, I am seldom repaid by gestures of kindness. Nor would I want to be, nor could I ever be. That is not the motivation behind the gift of love.

If I were, I'd be the loneliest priest in town. As far as young people are involved in my life, appreciation, mercifully, will never be an outward show of affection, a smothering of hugs and kisses, perhaps not even a surprise gift at Christmas, certainly, never a birthday card. The only time I get suspicious of a teenager is when she or he says, "Have a happy day." I feel I am about to be "had."

Again, I blush too easily at such signs of appreciation. I tend to choke up, or "lose it," as kids are wont to say. Yet there are signs of love, perhaps more body language than verbal — just being present, an approving wink, a bit of horseplay, a smile — little things that can mean a lot and be affirming. Unpredictable, not tangible. These gestures speak more than gifts.

Also, and I say this unashamedly, my young friends seem to sense that I need their companionship as much as they need my support. They lift my spirits, give me a playful, joyful approach to life which otherwise can be very burdensome. They ignite my priesthood, tap my inner resources, invite my creativity, invigorate my prayer life. That's a whole bunch of rewards right there.

In fact, it was the late Venerable John Henry Newman who believed that each of us needs to have demands made upon our daily sympathies and tenderness, needs to have someone to comfort, to consult, someone "to indulge the love of variety and the restless humors which are so congenial to the minds of most." In a word, we need friends to interplay and interact with us in order to grow in love.

My young friends do care for me, worry about my weight, help me overcome bad habits, and make sure I am always "The Priest." They don't want me to be anything else but first a priest. I must act like a priest, talk like a priest, and when I don't, they show their displeasure. It is a terrible responsibility.

Does that mean I can't be myself when I am around them? No, on the contrary they, are most comfortable when I am myself and not role-playing, not throwing my authority around, not putting on clerical airs.

It is difficult to separate the priest from the man. We are one person. We have our priestly functions and priestly robes, but we are also human beings, with all of our foibles and mannerisms, our virtues and vices. Lay people like to see and know the whole person, not just the cleric who wishes them "a happy day" in front of church on Sundays.

When my friend Michael Johnson introduced me to his friends, and he is not ashamed to do so, he presents me as "my priest." That's enough. His peers respect me from that moment on. I have gotten to know many of his friends.

When Michael was presented at a recent high-school football game on senior parents' night, his Aunt Betty Washington and I were introduced as his escorts. The crowd was amused when they saw this tall, black teen, made even larger by his equipment, walk across the field between the two of us. It was a proud moment for us all.

That was a gesture of appreciation on Michael's part, worth more to me than any gifts he could have bought me.

A Hot July in Lawndale

I REMEMBER arriving at Blessed Sacrament parish on July 4, 1966, to begin what would become a twelve-year pastoral experience on the west side of Chicago in the Lawndale community.

It was the summer of 1966. Doctor Martin Luther King, Jr., had brought his civil rights movement to Chicago and was planning peaceful, non-violent marches for open housing through all-white Cicero, which practically bordered on our parish boundaries. Dr. King was living not far away from us on Sixteenth Street.

On July 13 Chicago experienced its civil disorders. And the west side burned down. This was my parish.

Several days before the riots broke out, the pastor left for vacation. The other priests in the house were already on vacation, and I was strangely alone on my first assignment. Talk about Baptism by Fire! I'll never forget the helplessness and frustration and loneliness I experienced those days in a neighborhood in turmoil.

July 12, 1966, was a hot day in Chicago. Black youngsters were playing in water from an illegally opened fire hydrant when two police officers arrived at the scene and closed the hydrant. When a youth turned it on again, the police arrested him. A crowd gathered, and sporadic window-breaking, rock-throwing, and firebombing lasted for several hours. In Chicago, as in other cities, the long-standing grievance of the black community needed only a minor incident to ignite it.

On the evening of July 13, the day after the fire-hydrant incident, rock-throwing, looting, and firebombing began again. Before the police and 4,200 National Guardsmen managed to restore order, scores of civilians and police had been injured. There were 533 arrests, including 255 juveniles. Three blacks were killed by stray bullets, among them a 13-year-old boy and a 14-year-old pregnant girl.

One day during the riots I walked down Ogden Avenue, which crossed through our parish. It reminded me of bombed-out

Munich after World War II. The avenue with its gutted storefronts was a wasteland. Bottles were still being tossed from the rooftops when a squadron of police officers, guns drawn, pulled me over to ask what I was doing on the streets. "Get back to your rectory before you get killed," they ordered me.

I told them I was new to the area and was trying to know my parish. Walking though the war-torn area, I felt a terrible loneliness of not knowing the young people involved or any of the families affected.

What were the terrible hurts and frustrations and anger in these black youths to cause them to burn down and loot their own neighborhood? If anything like this happens again while I am here, I told myself, I want to know the young people involved. I want to know them by name. It was at this lonely moment on Ogden Avenue that I committed my priesthood to the young people of Lawndale. I spent the rest of the summer of 1966 quietly getting oriented to my role as priest in this community. Already plans began to form in my mind for reaching the youths with next summer's youth programs.

Chicago escaped civil disorders in the summer of 1967, but not the rest of the country. The worst came during a two-week period in July, first in Newark, then in Detroit. Each set off a chain reaction in neighboring communities. American cities were filled with shock, fear, and bewilderment.

On July 28, 1967, President Lyndon Johnson established the National Advisory Commission on Civil Disorders to find out what happened, why it happened, and what could be done to prevent it from happening again. The now famous Kerner Report was published in 1968. Its basic conclusion was that "Our nation is moving toward two societies, one black, one white — separate and unequal."

The Kerner Report decried the violence and destruction but insisted segregation and poverty, which created a destructive environment in the racial ghetto, must be ended, and it laid part of the blame at the doorsteps of white institutions that helped create the ghetto, maintain it, and condone it.

Finally, the Kerner Report called for new and high-impact

programs to close the gap between promise and performance and to undertake new initiatives and experiments that can change the system of failure and frustration that now dominates the ghetto and weakens our society.

Apostles in Lawndale

WHAT did the youthful Afro-Americans teach me in my twelve years in their midst? I ask this question as a priest and also as a man, not that the two can ever be separated in reality, only in reflection.

First, I was taught as a priest the beauty of celibacy, because without a commitment to celibacy I never would have met this exciting group of young Afro-Americans in the context of an inner-city parish assignment. I don't think they would have felt free to intertwine their lives with mine had I not made a strong commitment to celibacy in the service of the Church.

It was almost the total enmeshing of our lives for the twelve years on the west side of Chicago that made a lot of things happen in the parish and the Lawndale community of some two hundred thousand people. On the other side, through them and through their problems of growing up in a black ghetto, I came to feel and think and vibrate and pray with the poor. Their problems were symbolic — and still are today — of the poor, the dispossessed, the exploited young blacks in our ghettos.

I saw and felt the tensions in their lives — where there was a lack of role models for young black men and women — between the pull of becoming pimps, hustlers, drug dealers, and, if young women, welfare mothers where fathers were not or could not be present, or even known, and the pull to get an education, escape from the ghetto, and enter the middle class.

The street gangs did not want them to continue in school, but rather to join them in living in the streets. Their families, for the most part, insisted they remain in school, enter the job market, and get liberated from all the forces of drugs, crime, unemployment, and gangs.

My young black kids were caught up in these tensions, and if a celibate priest had not taken them by the hand and said, "Hey, there is a way out," I fear they would still be hanging around the street corners of the west side or in the jail or the morgue. Thousands like them are still "doing their thing in the streets" — without jobs or hope. We need only look at the recent census report on unemployed minority youths.

How to go about it was my concern, but the celibate love of Jesus showed me the way. I had the example of Jesus and the twelve to guide me. What these young people wanted was someone who cared, who believed in them, loved them as they were, and to find some opportunities for them to grow, lead, and move ahead despite the odds.

The practical means had to be tied to idealism — programs for reading and writing were as important as scholarships. How to apply for a job was as important as holding a job. How to lead a meeting was as important as running for political office. How to respect people and property was as important as how to celebrate the liturgy.

It all had to come together. What these youths taught me was that before I got entangled with their spiritual lives, I had to identify with their human lives. Too many preachers in the past have pacified black people with the "kingdom come" without showing them "The kingdom is already present." Christianity is not an escape from the world but a commitment to it. The black churches in America historically have been the center of civil rights movements and social change.

Not all of my apostles were Catholic — our Lawndale community was less than three percent Catholic — but don't let anyone tell them my little parish wasn't their church and that I wasn't their priest.

Through it all there has been a relationship much like what Jesus must have had with his apostles. One was a leader (I called him my "spiritual son"), like Peter, of an apostolic team of a dozen young people in my inner-city parish in the early 1970s. It was the Black Christian Students, a youth movement we were active in, destined to become city-wide as well as national during the late Sixties and early Seventies, when there was a rising interest in black power, black identity, black awareness. "Young, Beautiful, and Black" was our motto.

For about six years we were involved in all kinds of community-action programs on the west side of Chicago, many of them funded by the government, the Campaign for Human Development, Catholic Charities, and the elder Richard Daly, then mayor of Chicago. It embraced employment programs, job training, academic counseling, tutoring in reading and math, political action, neighborhood rehabilitation, gang control. It also included involvement of a small Catholic parish, Our Lady of Perpetual Help. We needed all the help we could get.

Through it all my twelve apostles grew in wisdom. My leader became the Joshua of the movement, as he was referred to — the right-hand man of Moses, who was trying to lead the young people to freedom. When he was turned on, everybody was turned on, especially the young ladies. When he was depressed, everyone was a downer. It wasn't easy for me to be Moses.

He and his brother apostles and I, for six years, screamed and yelled, fought, broke up furniture, but we also prayed together, broke bread together, and loved one another very deeply. It had to be the same way with Jesus and his twelve, I am convinced.

As a postscript, my apostles are now forty years old or over. Among my twelve, I number an advertising executive, two state representatives in Illinois, from the west side, a medical doctor, a lawyer and teacher of criminal law at Chicago State University, a Chicago educator, a community organizer, a police commander.

Some one should write the "Acts of the Apostles" of Lawndale.

Confessions of a Gang Leader

FACT: Coy Pugh, thirty-nine, is executive director of the West Side Small Business Development Corp., Chicago. He is also a political activist on the West Side.

Fact: Pugh, after his third term in prison for drug-related

crimes, began a successful transition in 1982 to a drug-free life.

Fact: This writer met Pugh in 1966 when he was fifteen years old and leader of the Cermak Deuces street gang in North Lawndale. Newly ordained, I was assigned to Blessed Sacrament Church in Lawndale where we organized the Black Christian Students. I met Pugh through our BCS activities. For the next twenty-four years our lives have intertwined.

Fact: I published a book, *You Got It All*, in 1980 that documented my work with young people in Lawndale through the Black Christian Students. Pugh was a part of the story. He read the book while serving time in Joliet State Penitentiary and credits the book with giving him a plan of action to make a transition to community action on the West Side of Chicago.

What follows is Pugh's story as he recently shared it with me for publication.

"When I first met you in 1966 at Blessed Sacrament, my identity problem, a common problem of young men who have not had proper role models or a father image in the home, first surfaced. I was reaching for straws to find out who I was and what I wanted to be. I was fifteen years old.

"When I was nine, my father left home. I was rebellious. I had never been close to my father. He never held me. My memories of him are negative — either as an alcoholic or as a mechanic who always was dirty, greasy, and who never smiled. I tavern-hopped with him when I was seven to nine years old, and he would give me liquor to introduce me to a man's world.

"Role models I look back on were drug dealers, pimps, and gang leaders. At fourteen or fifteen I showed some signs of charisma in leading others. In rebellion I began leading them against what society said was right — because society had no place for us as we saw society. No comfort zone.

"When we walked to school (Farragut High School) we had to walk through gang areas, either Hispanic or black gang turf. If we didn't join, we had to pay.

"Our solution was to start our own gang, the Cermak Deuces. Eventually we had five hundred members (we combined with the Soul Brothers farther west), and I became the leader.

"Our rival gang was the Vice Lords on Sixteenth Street.

"That's around the time we first met. You were running a storefront youth center at 3616 W. Cermak, where the Deuces often hung out. I recall the time you forged a truce between our gang and the Vice Lords at a stormy meeting at the rectory.

"We always had guns with us when we came to your Black Christian Students meetings in the rectory basement. You didn't know it. We also hid our guns in the storefront — a safe place, since it was church property. We were on marijuana then. No hard drugs came to Chicago till later.

"At fifteen I had left home and began living in the streets, trying to find a comfort zone where I could belong. It took me fifteen years to find out 'it ain't hip to be cool.' "

(Fact: I enrolled Pugh and his friend in St. Mel High School, at age seventeen, but the experiment was short-lived. They were expelled after three months.)

"My problem at St. Mel's was 'it was straight.' At Farragut I was the leader of five hundred gang members. I was somebody. At St. Mel's the Brothers whipped me. I couldn't adjust. I was back on the streets and hanging out in bars where drugs were sold and where I first tried heroin. It was in a dirty basement, with water from a gas station, at $3 a bag of capsules. We shot it with dirty needles. For a moment I felt euphoria. I found myself and what I was looking for. I found my comfort zone. After the high, reality set in.

"Now I had to get $21 a day for more bags, so I could get high again. Not by work, but by stealing. The more I used, the more I wanted. I had now withdrawn from society, slipped into another world without laws and restraints. I was in a lifestyle of hustling that began at six P.M. By midnight, you are high with illusions of grandeur. Life will be beautiful tomorrow. Drugs tell you this. Everything is cool. You are in control.

"I am considered a three-time loser in prison. I was always a poor criminal. I was burned by a cigarette on my first theft. When the gang shoved me through a window in my only robbery, a huge guy met me on the inside and wrestled me for my gun. I was driving a friend's rental car and was arrested for car theft.

"I began selling narcotics at seventeen and went to jail when my girl turned out to be an informant. I spent eighteen months in Milan, Michigan."

(Fact: When Pugh came out of Milan I enrolled him in DePaul University, but it only lasted a few weeks and then he was back on the streets.)

"At DePaul I couldn't make the transition to the straight world. I was wearing my zoot suit with wide lapels to theology classes. I went back to the streets. Then cocaine came around 1970. Cocaine does something to your body even sex can't achieve.

"But it also destroys your mind and your will, till all you think about is getting high. You don't want to continue, because after the first hit the highs level off, but you have lost your will to say no. What will I do as an alternative?

"For quite a few years in the Seventies, I was The Man. But my role models were still my peers in the streets — sick, dirty, unkempt hair. I got to a point where I didn't mind being in jail. I was a leader of my tier. I didn't have to make hard choices about drugs.

"My last time in Joliet, 1982, I began turning my life aground. As a last resort, I turned to Jesus. All else had failed. I began reading the Bible, then I began carrying the Bible, and I began discussing the Scriptures with everyone. I started going to prayer service. Some guys who knew me began to change. I was carrying Jesus' flag now, not the gang's.

"Then it happened, our friend Art Turner [state representative from the west side and first president of the Black Christian Students] sent me a copy of your book *You Got It All*. And there it was in the book — my road map for the future. You wrote about outsiders ripping off the ghetto, starting businesses, and providing inferior goods and services. You challenged us to take over the businesses. That became my plan for the future. I spent days working out my plan. I now found a way to use my life.

"When I got out of jail, I launched the small business economic development corporation on the West Side. Since 1985 I have been drug free. It has been a struggle, but I gave up cigarettes, alcohol, and drugs, and have become a vegetarian. I don't have the desire anymore.

"I try to explain to recovering narcotic users how we must see drugs as a poison, not as a treatment for our problems. Drugs can stop us from being all we can be. Narcotics are a crutch."

(Fact: Coy Pugh was elected to the Illinois House of Representatives for the Tenth District in the 1992 general elections.)

Being Yourself

WE sat in a quiet neighborhood restaurant one evening for dinner — this young urban Afro-American and I — as we are often wont to do. Our relationship has grown this past year, as I have tried to be supportive of him in his high-school endeavors.

It has meant many trips back and forth to our local high school for athletic and extracurricular activities. It has meant tutoring sessions and countless trips to McDonald's and to shopping malls.

It has meant almost a total commitment. Sometimes you roll the dice with potentiality when you see it in someone. I like to believe my judgment is good, after some thirty years in youth work, mostly among young black men in their high-school and college years.

Tonight was troubling because the young man, just turned sixteen, was troubled. Despite our close relationship, I seemingly was unable to penetrate his sullenness. Parents and youth counselors know full well how difficult it is to communicate with teens today (maybe it has always been thus), despite what one might think is a loving, caring relationship. Peers they will talk with, but adults — well, that is another story.

We sat in stony silence, and we ate in silence, and yet I knew he was troubled. I had seen it for a month.

Finally, on an inspiration from the holy Spirit, toward the end of our meal, I said, "Do you believe in fortune tellers?" I don't know where the thought came from. But he smiled and said, "Yes." I asked him if he wanted me to tell his fortune. He said, "Yes," again, and I took my used place mat, turned it over, and took pen in hand. Then I said, "Let us bow our heads in prayer. What Jesus tells me I will put down on paper."

Then, I hastily wrote a somewhat lengthy account. The first page started with a bunch of "ifs": "If you grow up naturally and enjoy your youth and not try to become an adult too soon . . . if you let your beautiful personality shine forth and not be so sullen . . . if you let people into your life to love you and not build barriers around your ego in relationships . . . if you break down the walls of your heart, learn how to love and display your emotions . . . if you be yourself and not try to be another . . ."

Then came the fortune: ". . . then you will be a lovable person and develop many loving relationships. You will love and be loved, and you will be able, through love, to be everything you are capable of being. You will be you and it will be beautiful to behold. The whole world awaits you."

Well, he read it, crumpled it and left it in the glove compartment. We drove silently into the night.

It is now six weeks. We have had some wonderful experiences together since that evening. Tonight we were coming back from McDonald's. I said to him, "Do you remember the night I told your fortune?"

"Yes," he responded, and added, "Whatever happened to that piece of paper? I kind of forgot what you said."

I told him that it had all come true. "I am very proud of you and pleased with you." He smiled broadly.

I told him the paper was back at the rectory, and we would go back and reread it. We did, and he looked solemn for a moment, then looked deep into my eyes. "Thanks," he said, and I took him home. We felt very close to each other at that moment.

The Joyful Gift of Tony

ONCE you turn sixty-five, you really don't care what people say or think about you. By then your reputation is pretty well made. You are who you are, and you know it.

As a sixty-five-and-over, I am having the time of my life

through a warm-hearted father-son-type relationship with Tony, a teenage Afro-American youth who most recently crossed my path in Chicago.

As a kind of odd couple, we cause joy and laughter wherever we go. Restaurants are one of our favorite haunts, where we love to do a kind of comedy routine, primarily to bring some joy into the often dreary life of a waitress.

It is all very spontaneous. We don't plan it as such, but we have such a good time together, enjoying each other's company and continually trying to outwit each other at table, that it becomes contagious. Soon, everyone sitting near us becomes involved, especially those who wait on us. One waitress nearly lost her job when she sat down at table with us — a "no no" in the business.

There is nothing but pure joy and laughter in our relationship, and even the most bored table person soon melts under our frivolity.

Tony may be only a teenager, but he is very mature, and a growing boy most people take for much older. If I see someone kind of staring at us, I usually make some remark like, "Don't be surprised that he is taller than I am. You see, his parents are over seven feet tall." That usually disarms them, because it wasn't his height that confused them, but rather the fact that he is black and I am white, a priest, and old enough to be his grandfather.

We draw similar types of reactions when we go shopping together, or work out at a local health club. No one can figure out the strange combination. And of course, we enjoy putting people on. When we were shooting pool together, one man called Tony over and said I was trying to hustle him. When I went with him at Christmas time to an all-women's store to buy a present for his girlfriend, it was an unusual sight to see a priest and a black teenager in an all-white suburban shopping mail. I ended up getting a clerical discount on his purchase, although the clerk said they didn't have too many priests coming through.

Part of our secret is that we both have a good sense of humor, are seldom out of sorts, generally free from mood swings, or if we have them, they soon pass away. Our affection for one another takes over.

It is a caring relationship that people can't fail to observe, and that is the secret of our joy. It rubs off on others. Clerks want us to come back and visit them, and if we do, they remember everything that happened the last time we were there — the fun we had together with the clerk. Tony especially is a very charismatic person. No one ever forgets him.

Tony has brought me more joy and happiness the last few years than I have a right to enjoy at my age. I thank God each day for the joyful gift of Tony. I feel much younger and am blessed to have someone to love and care for me.

John Henry Newman once wrote that we need close, intimate friends, if only to draw out virtues from within ourselves and express feelings and good wishes that otherwise we would never express. I feel that way about Tony. He draws the best out of me.

This is not exactly a new experience for me. Over the past twenty-five years, from the day of my ordination, I have raised a number of spiritual "sons," not legally adopting them but taking care of them. They have all come from the inner city and for the most part have not had an active father image during their adolescent years. I have tried in a small way to provide a positive male and father image.

All of these have developed into lasting friendships and relationships that exist yet today. Some of the young men are now close to forty years old, some of them are in the early twenties, and now Tony is an eighteen-year-old senior in high school. Each is unique in my life, and each has helped me to lead a balanced, fulfilled life. Each has tried to keep me from growing old, and has succeeded. Now it is Tony's turn.

Recently, a group of one hundred twenty priests gathered together to discuss sexuality and spirituality. It was all about the need of intimacy in our lives. One question posed was, "What kind of old man do you envision yourself?" For me, the question was moot. At sixty-eight I already had a wonderful family of young men who call me Dad. And I have a grandchild that calls me "Grandpa Geese."

I know what fun I am going to have as a celibate old man. These kids will always keep me young in heart, joyful, playful, and I don't fear loneliness, nor expect to become a dried-up, crochety priest.

I am sure when Jesus was traveling along the dusty roads of Galilee with his young disciples, it wasn't all religion. There had to be a lot of bantering and clowning around, displays of affection, cookouts along the road, some horseplay, and probably some games and sports. It had to be a happy, playful, joyful relationship that Jesus was building. Jesus was too loving a person not to have experienced all these genuine emotions and so build a loving, intimate relationship with the twelve.

God provided Tony for me when I had a disabling stroke. He was there to nurture me back to health. And for that reason, I dedicate this book to him.

PART THREE:
Putting on the Shoes of the Gospel

No Place to Lay Our Head

Whether in Southeast Asia, Central America, Eastern Europe, the Middle East, or Africa, refugees share a common suffering and alienation. They also share the biblical faith of old approved by God. They are the heirs of the same promise given to Abraham and dwell in the same tents with Isaac and Jacob. Unwittingly, they are searching for a heavenly home.

Refugees — even the Holy Family shared the refugee experience when they fled into Egypt to escape violence — are uprooted people, far from home and family. Refugees are impoverished, having abandoned all meager belongings when they left their homes; they are frightened, especially women and children, victims of violence at home, now fearful of what might befall them in a new, often unfriendly environment.

Refugees are aliens, strangers, foreigners, prisoners of refugee camps or ghettos, restless, lonely, friendless, and culturally adrift. Refugees are often hungry, sick, ill-housed, unclothed, without schools and hospitals, in a real sense at the mercy of people they do not know or governments they do not trust.

If there are feelings of inferiority, lack of self-respect, or identity crises, surely refugees experience them most profoundly. All their aspirations of founding a family, charting a career, or completing an education are put on hold in a refugee camp. Their only reality is survival.

"By acknowledging themselves to be strangers and foreigners on the earth, they showed that they were seeking a homeland. If they had been thinking back to the place from which they had come, they would have had the opportunity of returning there. But they were searching for a better, heavenly home" (Hebrews 11:13-16).

How do these observations relate to the liturgical season of Lent? For the refugees, the cry of the Church for penance, prayer, sacrifice, and almsgiving must ring a bit hollow. Refugees don't need a special season of the year for Lenten practices; they are already suffering, sacrificing, praying, and hoping. Their whole life is a prolonged Lent in anticipation of a new life promised at Easter by the resurrection of the Lord.

From my experience in interviewing countless refugees, there is more joy, hope, expectation, gratitude to God, and sharing in a refugee camp than in most of our civilized Western communities. To this extent, refugee camps give silent witness to the rest of the world on what the season of Lent is all about. Refugees silently call us to a deeper Christian life of service to the dispossessed of the world and make our meager offerings, sufferings, prayer, and almsgiving during Lent more meaningful.

Refugees at the spiritual level symbolize for us the life described in the New Testament for all who would embrace Jesus and his Church. As Christians, we too are aliens, foreigners, displaced persons, whose home is not in this world. We too are lonely, alienated, disoriented by sin, an enslaved people en route to our permanent, eternal home with our Father in heaven.

We too, like the Lord, have no place to lay our heads and are destined to suffer and die with Christ during the season of Lent in order to rise with him on Easter and return home, resurrected with new life, fully liberated.

If we search our own personal lives, we will find how much we are with our refugee brothers and sisters. In one way or another, we are all refugees sojourning through life. We are pilgrims without a permanent home.

On Ash Wednesday 1980, I was standing ankle-deep in ashes in a burned-out refugee camp at Nong Khai, Thailand, along the Mekong River separating Thailand from Laos. Some seven thousand Laotian refugees had been burned out by a ravaging fire, once again homeless and dispossessed, fortunate to escape the fire with their families, but with all possessions lost, including precious papers that might one day provide an opportunity to go to a Third-World country.

I wondered what a priest would say to them this Ash Wednesday about the meaning of Lent, self-sacrifice, sin, reconciliation, suffering, death, and resurrection. Yet there was no anger in their voices, no sadness on their faces. There was a certain resignation to the hardships of life.

The fire was just one more obstacle along the way to freedom. For many, the long trek from their farms, villages, and towns to escape the Pathet Lao government had already been filled with hardship, loss, hunger, disease, fear, and separation from loved ones. They had suffered much already, and the fire was one more roadblock to freedom. It was something they could live with. At least their families were still intact.

On Ash Wednesday 1981, I found myself in Central America visiting a Salvadoran refugee camp in Honduras along the border at Colomoncagua. All along the Western border of Honduras in the provinces of Octotepeque, Limpira, Intibuca, and La Paz, the refugees from oppression in El Salvador were fleeing the ravages of civil war in El Salvador. More than 25,000 had already arrived: others were going to Nicaragua, Costa Rica, Panama, and Mexico.

Once again we were in the midst of a frightened people who had fled violence and death in their own country, a simple peasant people whose only hopes were for peace and enough land to support their families. Two years later they were still huddled in refugee camps along the Honduran border, still suffering, hoping for peace, praying for a return to their ancestral land.

On Ash Wednesday 1982, I was in Vienna, Austria, visiting Polish refugees, some forty thousand who had fled Poland before the imposition of martial law the previous December and now were awaiting an opportunity to come to a third country to start life anew. Many of them were simply waiting to return to Poland.

This Ash Wednesday, February 16, 1983, I will be in Beirut, Lebanon, hopefully visiting Palestinian refugee camps, reporting on that part of the refugee world. Without my planning it, the Lord had led me over four years to refugee camps in Southeast Asia, Central America, Europe, and the Middle East to mark the beginning of Lent. I wonder where he will lead me next year.

The decade of the Eighties has been designated the Decade of the Refugee, and it reminds us that we are pilgrims without a permanent home, "restless until we rest with thee, O Lord." That, I believe, is the true meaning of Lent.

Along the Mekong River: 1980

ALONG the northern border of Thailand, just across the Mekong River, the camp of Ban Vinai is home for 32,500 Hmong tribesmen from the mountains of Laos. Most Hmongs, who only 200 years ago fled China to the mountains of Laos and Thailand, hope to go to the United States or to China.

Fiercely independent, the Hmong hill tribes have fought against the Vietnamese (on the side of the United States) from 1960 until 1975. Now they are holding out in mountain villages against the Pathet Lao (Vietnamese-backed regime).

They are farmers: opium is their money crop. They are fighters. They bring their women and children to Thailand, but the men want to go back to Laos and fight.

Khao I Dang is new and huge, but it is well-organized and stabilized.

Less than six months old, this holding center for Kampuchean refugees was thrown up quickly under emergency conditions last fall when thousands of starving, dying, and diseased Cambodians streamed across to the Thai border barely twelve kilometers away.

There are now 110,000 Cambodian refugees in this holding center — called a holding center, not a refugee camp, because these 110,000 people have no refugee status with either the Thai government or the United Nations. They are displaced persons, illegal aliens, and thus are eligible for a third-country sponsorship.

With another impending famine in Cambodia, it is possible that still another 400,000 or more starving refugees will cross into Thailand before the monsoon season begins in late May.

Khao I Dang is in stable condition now. Starvation, disease, and malnutrition are being eliminated in the camp, and children are beginning to smile and sing and play again. Outside of Khao I Dang, at the border between Thailand and Cambodia, just twelve kilometers away, thousands of Cambodians are near the border and in need of mammoth relief programs.

Famine in East Africa: 1980

WHEN our chartered Cessna put down near the tribal village of Kakuma in Turkana, some six hundred miles north of Nairobi, capital of Kenya, we were suddenly in another world which is literally untouched by modern civilization.

At this remote outpost of darkest Africa, not far from the Uganda border to the West and Sudan to the North, few residents have seen a paved road, used a knife or fork, watched TV, and tasted piped water or Coca Cola.

The vast arid area of the Turkana province, nearly the size of Ireland, is centered around the Turkana River, now run dry. A severe drought has gripped the area the past three years, and some quarter-million Turkani are plagued by famine.

Nearly all the cattle of these cattle-herding nomads have died, and until recently cholera was rampant.

This arid desert area knows intense heat, up in the hundreds during the day with cooler winds at night; now nearly all vegetation is dried up, and the people come to the Turkana river bed to dig holes for water for drinking, cooking, and bathing. It is the contaminated water that has created much of the disease.

Almost inaccessible by roads — at least a three-day journey by car — Turkana is best reached by charter plane. As our plane moved out of the fertile highlands around Nairobi, a beautiful modern city of 800,000 in the South of Kenya, en route to Turkana, we flew over volcanic mountain ranges into the flat, remote, arid area.

Kaukuna, a tribal village, is the site of a Catholic mission where we were to stay several days. It is one of several Catholic missions in the diocese of Lodwar, established only two years ago

— a diocese consisting of an Irish bishop, fourteen missionary priests, twelve religious sisters and some thirty lay volunteers.

It is only since 1963, when Kenya obtained its independence from English colonial rule, that white people have been allowed in Turkana, previously a closed area. The new government of Jomo Kenyatta invited the Catholic missionaries in to assist in relief work in the aftermath of a severe drought in 1961, but not until 1963 were they allowed to do apostolic work.

Since 1968 the Catholic Church has prospered in this desolate area. There are some twenty thousand Catholics in the Lodwar diocese, which includes all of Turkana, and in the Kakuma mission (and its outpost at Nanan some fifty kilometers away) there are nearly four thousand.

The Kakuma mission receives help from Germany and Ireland as well as England. Catholic Relief Services supplies food and medicine, sponsoring development programs in hygiene and child care.

Some 3,500 children, most of them preschoolers, are taken care of at the Catholic mission. Many of them live at the mission or commute sporadically if their families live nearby. The mission provides a network of seven nursery schools, with 400 to 900 students in each school, very primitive, with small thatched classrooms scattered throughout the area, under the supervision of an African teacher, and with centralized feeding stations.

Most of the children are badly nourished, with thin arms and legs but protruding stomachs caused by tapeworms. Many suffer glaucoma from the constant blowing of dust in their eyes and from poor hygiene, but only the seriously sick are cared for in the mission hospital.

Father Bernard Ruhnau is a forty-seven-year-old German missionary, who has been at Kaukuna some eight years. He totally identifies with the people and currently takes care of the mission at Nanan. Father Bernard lives with an extended tribal family in their *manyatta* — a cluster of thatched huts, where he sleeps in the open on a dried hide and eats their food: camel's milk, dried beans, the blood of cattle. He has a small store of supplies there, including petrol for the mission's Land Rover. There is a small parish house in Nanan, but Father Bernard celebrates Mass outdoors with a lively Catholic liturgy incorporating local music and customs with full participation.

Father Desmond Miller heads the Catholic Mission at Kakuma, but he works closely with Father Bernard in fraternal support. We stayed at the modest but comfortable parish house in Kakuma. There is also a large church at Kakuma, built four years ago.

As we bumped along for nearly a hundred miles through the mission in the Land Rover, the two missionaries talked about their work.

The primary work of the Catholic mission now is response to the drought and famine. Five months ago, before Catholic Relief Services began to supply milk, wheat, and cooking oil, cholera was rampant, and Father Desmond buried thirty children in one week. All that has been reversed now as the feeding stations begin to show their good effects. But there is no end in sight for the drought. Wells have to be dug, irrigation and reforestation are needed, and all kinds of development projects must be initiated.

Church Suffering in Central America: 1981

BISHOPS, brother priests, religious sisters, and Christian laity are suffering a great deal these days in Central America, some to the point of martyrdom. This is especially true in El Salvador, Guatemala, to some extent in Honduras, and even in Costa Rica. Fortunately, the revolution is complete in Nicaragua, and that country is relatively at peace.

To rub salt in their sufferings, some American, even Catholic, media, and at times state department spokesmen, malign their reputations, are suspect of their motives, and even question their commitment to the poor.

On a recent visit to Central America to get eyewitness accounts, where I interviewed countless priests and religious in Nicaragua, Honduras, and Costa Rica, and still others exiled from El Salvador and Guatemala, I sensed the sufferings the Church is experiencing, but through it all, as one Jesuit in Honduras expressed it, there is great hope for the Church and a sense of renewal of faith among the people.

Sometimes we fail to appreciate the dilemma so many of our brother and sister religious are facing in carrying out their intense pastoral mission in poor rural and urban barrios jam-packed with marginated people. This is their mission, where they are working out their "fundamental option for the poor," according to the directives of Puebla and Medellin. Many of them are missionaries from other countries, whether the United States, Canada, Europe, or wherever. They have been invited to Central America because of a shortage of native priests and sisters.

In 1946, for example, the Honduran bishops, through Propagation of the Faith, invited the Jesuits to take care of the entire 600-square-mile territory of Yoro, where today they are serving 90,000 baptized Catholics spread throughout El Progreso and 110 small villages and towns inhabited by poor campesinos.

The Church in Central America is grateful for this enormous contribution, as Bishop Rivera Damas said to bishops of New York in a recent visit. "Your solidarity with the Church of El Salvador is greatly appreciated. Your concern is not in words. You have sent your own sons and daughters to work among the poor and the oppressed in my country. You have even spoken out against the policy of your government of sending military supplies to El Salvador that only can be used for more violence and bloodshed."

But now missionary priests and sisters are being persecuted for their work with the poor, for putting shoes on the Gospel, as martyred Jesuit Father Rutilo Grande from El Salvador expressed it. Priests and sisters are considered revolutionaries, leftists, enemies of the state, and placed on military hit lists. They are followed, harassed, intimidated, sometimes killed or mutilated for "their fundamental option for the poor."

The degree of their involvement varies, of course. Some have joined the revolution completely to be with their people; some keep a nonpolitical stance, despite their deep commitment to the poor. Very often it depends upon the person and the situation.

What remains true, however, is that these dedicated men and women are doing pastoral work. Very often their involvement with the simplest human and social development programs, such as cooperatives, unions, refugees, or Christian base communities, has labeled them, in the eyes of rightist military governments, as suspect, dangerous, even as Marxists. So they are harassed. Many have been exiled, denied their residency passes, sent back home.

So the dilemma remains. How to be aligned with the poor and the oppressed and still avoid government harassment? Whence the suffering, the cross, the martyrdom, the fears. Identification with the poor has resulted in persecution, massacre, rape, mutilation, death. We need only recall Archbishop Oscar Romero, or the three American sisters and lay volunteers of recent memory. I was told that many lay catechists and delegates of the Word also are suffering and dying for their faith.

Archbishop Romero lived with the threat of death. He said shortly before his assassination, "I have frequently been threatened by death. I must say to you as a Christian, I don't believe in death without resurrection. If thy kill me, I will rise again in the people of El Salvador. I say this to you in humility, not pride."

It is an oversimplification to reduce all these tensions to a confrontation between Marxist Cuban guerrillas on the one side, and military rightists on the other side. The Democratic Liberation Fronts in Nicaragua, El Salvador, and Guatemala are broadly based coalitions of campesinos, Indians, workers, teachers, students, Christian base groups, and political factions, including the Communist party. They are popular fronts supported by guerrilla military units, which are often fighting among themselves and have been Cuba-trained.

The poor and oppressed campesinos are not interested in ideologies, but in justice and redistribution of the land, so that the years-old gap between the rural poor and the wealthy families and transnationals can be closed. That's what the revolution is all about. Governments have come and gone, but the plight of the people seems never to change.

This is why the Church in El Salvador, for example, did not want military aid sent into their country from either East or West, either the U.S. or the [former] USSR. What is needed is peaceful dialogue to bring an end to civil war, along with massive economic aid to help these poor countries get back on their feet.

Over and over I heard the plea that peace without justice is meaningless. It is not a matter of one side winning or one side losing a bitter internal war. It is a matter of self-determination, a matter of social justice. Neither the U.S. nor the Soviets can be allowed to use these small nations as a staging ground for global ideological battles between capitalism and socialism.

Interestingly enough, in Guatemala, which is ripe for revolution, it is the Indians, comprising fifty-five percent of the population and exploited for decades, who are kicking up their heels. No longer passive and long-suffering, they have become politicized and revolutionary, but they are neither Marxist nor Christian. They are simply angry with the system. If anything, they are more sympathetic to the Church than to Cuba or Russia.

The threat of revolution, accentuated by the successful Sandinista overthrow of Somoza in Nicaragua in 1979, the current revolution in El Salvador, and the heating up in Guatemala, have increased tensions in Honduras and Costa Rica. The military provisional government in Guatemala and the democratic government of Costa Rica both are closing in on human rights and moving to the right as a result of what is happening in El Salvador. The Church will surely be put to the test in these countries as well.

We priests and religious in North America must be in solidarity with our brothers and sisters in Central America. We must develop a solidarity between our Church and their Church, our people and theirs. It will never be a popular cause, but then, persecutions never are.

The Raping of a People: 1982

IT is the fear of torture, mutilation, death, the looting of their homes, the raping of their children, and the destruction of their villages that drives Guatemalan refugees — most of them Indians — across the border into the department of Chiapas in Southern Mexico.

They carry with them scars of the horror they witnessed or that members of their families suffered. They come to Mexico — 180,000 strong, some of them probably temporary workers, perhaps 80,000 or more remaining in Chiapas.

To date only two centers of so-called legal aliens are recognized by the Mexican government — El Sombro and La Marca — along the Mexican-Guatemalan border of the municipality of Trinitoria with some fifteen hundred refugees.

Here these refugees cling to the many hills in Southern Mexico in clusters of thatch-roofed huts — perhaps as many as forty thousand dotting the forty hills — but getting figures on Guatemalan refugees is difficult at best because so many refugees hide away in the hills and prefer to scratch out their living unknown to government authorities.

No so the Guatemalan Indians in El Sombro and La Marca. Through the intervention of the Catholic bishops of Chiapas, who issued a pastoral statement on the refugee situation in February, the Mexican government declared the refugees at El Sombro and La Marca legal for three years, but they must renew their legal status every three months. Illegals are subject to be returned to Guatemala, often meaning certain death.

Most of these Guatemalans left because of the general climate of terror but have difficulty showing concrete proof of persecution.

Such technical and legal issues are beyond the concerns of these simple campesinos and Indians scattered along the border. Whoever is channeling the food, they say they aren't getting very much out of it. A leader of the camp says they need beans, rice, sugar, salt, and soup — basics for the 120 families (1,400 people) at the Buena Vista campsite we visited in El Sombro. If the food could be trucked as far as Las Delicias, he said, the refugees would bring it the rest of the way by oxcarts.

Meanwhile, they continue to work very small plots of ground (which they do not own) at the foot of the hills to raise what they can for themselves. If anything, these refugees from terror have seemingly been abandoned by both the Mexican government and private humanitarian agencies. They feel isolated, since they are not wanted either in Guatemala or in Mexico, and many who have tried to return home were quickly met with torture or death.

February 2, 1981, more than four hundred Guatemalans were expelled from the zone of Montebello.

February 7, 1981, officials began rounding up and deporting refugees from Comalapa.

April 25, 1981, more than four hundred refugees were deported from Campeche. (According to later testimony, those refugees were turned over to the Guatemalan army. Later they were shut up in a military post in Camejaito, where the men "disappeared" and afterward the women and children were given away.)

July 26, 1981, two thousand persons were expelled from the Lacandona jungle.

January 11, 1982, more than seven hundred persons from the camp of Dolores were obliged to cross the border. They were barely beginning to cross when a helicopter of the Guatemalan army began to fly overhead.

In the zone of Comalapa, one sees continuous transit of immigration vehicles, hunting down refugees. In February and March of last year, the officials charged a hundred-peso bribe not to return Guatemalans to their country. In September and October, the amount had risen to five hundred and soon as high as a thousand, probably because there weren't as many refugees.

As the refugees live with the constant threat of being returned to Guatemala, their highest priority is the legalization of their military situation. For this it is necessary to pressure the Mexican government, so that they sign the United Nations protocol on refugees; thus, it is could be easier for the refugees to legalize their stay in Mexico.

As one philosophically gestured, "I'd sooner be killed cleanly by one Mexican bullet than mutilated, tortured, then killed in Guatemala." But the situation seems relatively calm in Southern Mexico at present. Perhaps the rainy season has made the area too inaccessible. One thing is evident. The refugees cling to the Mexican side of the hills for security, not the Guatemalan side.

The refugees we talked to are relatively content in Mexico, while they hope one day to return to Guatemala in peace. The recent coup d'état in Guatemala, which established Rios Montt, a born-again Christian, as a strongman dictator, has not stopped the violence and terror in the rural areas of Guatemala. To date, the rugged campesinos see little improvement in the climate of terror in their country, and are not hopeful for the future.

Several I spoke with talked freely of the terror in Guatemala which they experienced or witnessed. Soldiers come into the village to pillage it, kidnap and torture the people — even children are tortured and murdered, especially the Indians. One cited witnessing three men who were tortured, hanged, and shot. Finally, they were tied, castrated, and floated down the river. They also cited examples of what happened to those who returned to Guatemala. Finally, they told stories of pregnant women being split open at the abdomen, and soldiers in numbers up to six hundred gang-raping twelve- and thirteen-year-old girls.

In one village the soldiers came with gifts of toys and candy for the children, clothes for the women, then cordoned off the village, and killed all the men within earshot of their families.

Prior to their pastoral statement, the bishops of Chiapas had visited the camp at La Marca and appealed for elemental human rights for the refugees. The day the bishops issued their pastoral letter, there was a coup d'état in Guatemala. Two catechists returned to Guatemala after the coup and were murdered. Some forty-five of seventy-five families who returned home are now back in Mexico. On the day of the coup, two thousand refugees crossed over into Mexico.

Sister Lucia and her co-worker Francisco, who accompanied us on our trip to the refugee camp, work with a diocesan committee established to deal with Central American refugees. Their commission expanded when Guatemala refugees began coming into Mexico in 1981. Catholic Relief Services funds their work.

Vast assistance programs are needed, and as these terrorized people flee into Mexico, the greater the need becomes. The raping of a people could very well end with the death of a nation.

El Sombro, Mexico: 1982

Y OGI Berra, noted for his aphorisms when catching for the New York Yankees, once made the profound observation that a baseball game is never over until it is over. On our recent trek through Southern Mexico to the Guatemala border in search of isolated Guatemalan refugees who had been frightened out of Guatemala into Mexico, I found the truth of Yogi's wisdom.

Mexican airlines had brought us from Chicago to Mexico City, whence we flew south to Tuxtla Gutiérrez in the department of Chiapas, Indian territory of Mexico. From Tuxtla we chartered a bus for an hour-and-a-half ride to San Cristóbal de las Casas, a delightful small city, which put us within range of the Guatemalan border some 200 miles away, of which 150 were on the Pan American highway. But below the city of Comitán we had to turn off for 50 miles of some of the roughest, rockiest, muddiest road ever carved by man, to El Sombro, where seven of the eight refugee colonies are scattered along the hillsides at the border.

The visit to the forlorn and forgotten refugees seemed destined for failure from the moment we arrived in San Cristóbal. We were advised, and by trusted Catholic Relief Service staffers from Mexico City, to cancel the trip. We were in the rainy season and roads were becoming impassible. We were told it would take us ten hours to get to El Sombro, the last twenty-five kilometers by foot. We were warned that Mexican military and government reps in the area would not let us into the camp area. We were told that roads were washed out. And we were assured that these scared Guatemalan Indians would not give a story or allow a picture to be taken.

It wasn't until we met a determined and absolutely fearless little Mexican nun — Hermana Lucia, whose mission is to the indigenous poor in Chiapas, especially the refugees — that we decided to push forward despite the odds. In fact, Sister Lucia and her coworker Francisco, who are part of a diocesan team in San Cristóbal, said they were going with us.

Not only was Sister Lucia knowledgeable — she had been to the border often — but she had more stamina than the rest of us put together. Three- or four-day trips by foot to the jungle area of Chapias are nothing out of the ordinary for this remarkable woman.

Off we went in two rented Volkswagens (we should have had Jeeps) on what turned out to be a four-hour ride by car (the last fifty kilometers over the terrible road, if there was a road, and the last five kilometers by foot up a winding hillside in the heat of the afternoon). We had finally come to a mudhole along the road and had to abandon the cars and continue by foot, backpacking all of our movie and camera equipment. We were on an odyssey into the unknown wilds of Southern Mexico.

Like an oasis at the Guatemala border, we finally saw El Sombro in the distance, still a mile away down a ravine, through fields marked with barbed wire and across a stream. It looked like a mirage, not a tightly organized refugee tent city but a collection of bird's nests dotting the hillside on the Mexican side of the hill. Here they eked out a living on a small plot of ground not their own.

By four P.M. we were in a cluster of thatched-roof huts — called Buena Vista — at El Sombro, fast running out of good light for our cameramen. But we got in and out of the camp by five-thirty, and were back up the ravine for our five-kilometer trek back to our beaten-out Volkswagens. Sure enough, one of them would not start. So we taxied our eight-member team to the nearest village, Las Delicias, where we gathered at a small Catholic mission around nine P.M. — a refuge for us in a time of need.

We met the pastor, and unbelievable as it may sound, he was an American Maryhill missionary from San Antonio, Texas. Father David Perez had been in Guatemala for over five years. He had been chased out, and now was taking care of his mission near the border and reaching out to the refugees. Our Lady of Good Hope is the name of his mission.

Father Perez drove his jeep back to our abandoned car. A storm was gathering, and if we didn't get the car out that night, it might remain the rest of the rainy season. Miraculously, he got the car running and personally led our caravan two hours over rough roads to the good highway which would take us back to San Cristóbal by two A.M. We arrived back at our hotel hungry, tired, thirsty, and dirty, but full of good hope because the first leg of our visit to God's poorest at the borders of Central America was complete.

One final note: We never saw a military or government person along the way, and the refugees were very cooperative once they knew us. The trip took five hours each way, not ten; we only walked five kilometers each way, not twenty-five; and for the first time in two weeks, it hadn't rained for two days. Thank you, Sister Lucia.

Colomoncagua, Honduras: 1981

COLOMONCAGUA is a town of eight hundred souls right on the border between El Salvador and Honduras.

Last December, 1980, several weeks before Christmas, Salvadoran refugees fleeing military attacks by government troops began flooding into the area. Some two months later, there were 3,200 refugees mingled into this poor Honduran campesino area.

All along the western border of Honduras in the provinces of Octotepegue, Limpira, Intibuca, and La Paz, the refugees from oppression in El Salvador keep coming to escape the ravages of civil war tearing El Salvador apart.

In Colomoncagua they have swarmed into the churches, the schools, the marketplace, the countryside.

When the refugees first started coming in December, no one paid much attention. At first the government of Honduras — and the United States — pretended it wasn't happening. The violence inside El Salvador wasn't supposed to be.

Today there is an ecumenical effort in the Colomoncagua area. The United Nations office of the High Commissioner has poured $400,000 into the program, with another $1,300,000 earmarked for the first half of 1981.

Warehouses are being built to hold food supplies, clothing, and medicine being shipped in. Clinics have been thrown up; tent cities have been built on mountainsides. Little by little, aid is coming to these stricken people.

Sunday, February 22, we flew in a small Cessna plane courtesy of Wings of Hope from Tegucigalpa, the capital city of Honduras, to the western border of El Salvador. Landing on a small dirt strip at Concepción, we went by CRS jeep first to Camasca, to visit Father Luis Alonzo, pastor of 60,000 in the Camasca area, where more than 3,000 refugees are located in Colomoncagua, Santa Lucía, and San Antonio.

Father Luis gave me some altar wine and hosts to take to Colomoncagua, where I was to celebrate an afternoon Mass in the local church for the refugees and the Hondurans in the village. It is not too often a Mass is celebrated, so the four Honduran sisters, who are working there as medical aides, were delighted to have me come.

When we arrived at Colomoncagua, we were plunged into the refugee situation. The large parish church had become home for some 200 of the refugees. A tent city of 51 plastic tents on a mountainside had been built to house 573 refugees.

Colomoncagua, Honduras: 1982

ALEJANDRO Ortíz and his wife, Exaltación, will never forget January 20, 1977, the day their son, Father Ottavio Ortíz, was murdered at the San Antonio Abad retreat house in San Salvador, the capital of El Salvador.

For eighteen months now, the parents of Father Ottavio have been in this refugee camp across the Salvadoran border in Honduras. They are still awaiting peace in their country and an opportunity to return again to their home in the Morazón district of El Salvador.

After the murder of Ottavio, still another son, a mere sixteen-year-old, was also murdered, and they themselves were driven out of the country. Alejandro was suspect because he was a catechist, his wife told me. A daughter survives in El Salvador, but her children are in the refugee camp with their grandparents.

As we sat together this Sunday afternoon in their small tent on a makeshift bamboo bed, the couple wanted to talk about Ottavio, who was thirty-five years old when he was martyred. He had been a priest for five years.

Ottavio was not a "political" priest, but he was a part of a team of five priests who worked together in five parishes subdivided into sixteen base communities in San Salvador. Also he was the rector of the minor seminary, always considered suspect by the military, but for what reason they didn't know.

On January 20, 1977, at five A.M., a tank battered down the door of the diocesan retreat house, where Father Ottavio had brought forty-three students (fifteen to nineteen years old) the night before for a weekend course in Christian doctrine. The course began with a Mass the night before, at which Father Ottavio preached about making the blind see and reaching out to the poor, based on the Gospel of St. Luke.

The next morning, the government troops entered and killed Father Ottavio and four of the students. Not until late the next afternoon was there a government announcement that an armed battle was taking place between students and the armed forces at the retreat house. The soldiers said they were looking for arms, but all they found were song books and a guitar.

Archbishop Oscar Romero, archbishop of San Salvador, himself to be martyred two years later while celebrating Mass, came for the bodies and removed them to the Cathedral, where a wake service was conducted later that night. The cathedral was full. The rest of the children were forced to crawl on their elbows to safety. The soldiers remained in the retreat house for five days.

Archbishop Romero had wanted to bury his martyred priest from the cathedral to underscore the tragedy, but the family decided to bury him from the parish where Father Ottavio worked among the poor.

Alejandro Ortíz and his wife spoke freely about their hope for their stricken country. These simple campesinos want to go home. He said, "We hope to see you again someday in our country."

For peace to come to El Salvador, Alejandro said, El Salvador must be liberated from the military and from the "*Yanqui*" — the

United States — and secondly, "we must liberate ourselves from the injustices we inflict upon ourselves." He believes the revolutionaries want liberation for everyone. He is not so sure about the Christian Democrats (Duarte), and even less sure about the present ruling junta. "The Christian Democrats promised us peace with the elections, but we didn't believe them."

El Salvador is further from a truce now than even before the elections, but until there is a truce or a negotiated settlement, the country cannot rebuild. He hopes the free nations of the West will help negotiate a peace in El Salvador.

When we ended our visit, I told him how sorry I was about Ottavio's murder. Alejandro put his arms around me and wept. He said simply, "You are my son. You are a priest."

We bid farewell on a Sunday afternoon on a hillside near the Salvadoran border. Across that poorly marked border and beyond the hills of El Salvador the violence and oppression which has brought so much human suffering, especially to the poor, raged on.

Postscript: It is toward the end of 1986, I was once again visiting a center for Christian Formation in the parish of San Antonio Abad in San Salvador, where two Irish Sisters of St. Clair, one from St. Petersburg, Florida, the other from Ireland, do pastoral work.

I was startled when I saw a drawing of Father Ottavio Ortíz Luna and the four young men killed with him on the wall of the meeting room. The sisters told me it was at this very center that Father Ottavio and the boys were killed in 1979.

They knew his parents well because they had worked for eleven years in the war-torn area of Morazón when the fighting was at its worst in the early war years. In the town of Gutera, they fed fifteen thousand displaced persons daily for five years, under constant siege from the war and in constant personal danger. They told us of horror stories of massacres, crop burnings, and the destruction of villages. The war still wages in that area six years later.

It was a particularly touching moment for me to stand on the ground where Father Ottavio was killed.

Alejandro and his wife are still in the same refugee camp. The

Sisters are still working among the displaced. And the war still rages on.

'Putting Shoes on the Gospel'

I KEEP thinking about that nun on a mule in the Chinandega area of northwestern Nicaragua. How she rode that mule into the far reaches of this rural area of forty thousand campesinos who were without a doctor. How she came among them as a nurse to tend to their sick and teach them preventive medicine.

I called the parish in El Viejo a parish without a priest, but the six sisters working in this rural cotton-picking area look upon it as an area without a doctor. In both cases, the need is for healers of forty thousand people.

These Spanish Sisters of Mercy are nurses who train young men to be "promoters of health" in the area. They asked me to stay with them as their priest.

A story of healing in Chinandega, an almost forgotten area topping up into the northwest border of Honduras along the Pacific Ocean, the forty thousand scattered farmers raise cotton, sugar cane, and bananas on large private farms. The only hospital in the area is in the city of Chinandega and has a hundred fifty beds. Doctors have never visited the rural area, but these valiant sisters have been working in El Viejo for eight years in health outreach programs.

For thirty years the Vincentian Fathers manned the parish and worked with the people. The pastor died last August. The bishops of León sent the Vincentians home. It is a parish without a priest in a crisis too complex to explain here.

For too long before the revolution, the sisters rode their mules to outreach areas to care for the sick, with little or no time to teach preventive medicine. Now the "promoters of health" ride the mules, and the sisters train the young men.

It is an exciting program. We visited one of the outreach dispensaries in the middle of nowhere. Now if we can only send a priest to El Viejo to take on Christ's healing action.

I am terribly torn to go back there.

It wasn't easy under Somoza, and some of the National Guard still train across the border in Honduras, some say with American aid.

People died for lack of medical care — a boy bitten by a snake, a woman in childbirth. No doctors, only a nun on a mule.

But mules now have become horses, and soon there will be ambulances. It is the stubborn mule of a bishop we have to deal with.

"Putting shoes on the Gospel" — that's not my expression. Father Rutilio Grande, S.J., a Salvadoran priest working among the campesinos, who was ambushed by the security forces, coined it. His people still quote it.

I can't get the expression out of my mind.

That's what Jesus was all about. He was the "Gospel" incarnate. He carried it by foot and by mule through the campesino areas and villages of Palestine two thousand years ago.

Palestine and Central America aren't too much different, even the terrain, certainly the poverty, the sick, the oppressed. The Jews were being held hostage by occupation troops of the Roman Empire. The campesinos in El Salvador and Guatemala are being held hostage by oppressive military terrorists, right and left.

The Sunday I celebrated Mass among the Salvadoran refugees and Honduran peasants at Colomoncagua, an isolated village along the Salvadoran border, the Gospel text was all about turning the other cheek and praying for your persecutors.

What an apt text — and what a hard text for victims of oppression! Nevertheless I preached on it. "Jesus is the Lord of truth and justice. He will bring justice to the poor. We can't take retribution in our own hands. We must pray for our persecutors. Jesus hears the prayers of the poor."

In a way, an easy homily for me to give, for after the Mass, I left the area. I'm back in the U.S.A. now, physically far removed from the nun on a mule, from the grave sites of three sisters and a lay volunteer ravaged in El Salvador, a year removed from the martyrdom of Archbishop Romero; long gone from the refugee camp at Colomoncagua, although only three hours by plane from

Central America, its oppression, poverty, bullets, and fears.

But I can't forget.

It is Palm Sunday. Jesus is riding his mule into Jerusalem. His shoes are walking the Gospel into Jerusalem, where this week he himself will be put to death for his hard sayings, for his commitment to the poor, for his passion for justice.

The Romans will judge him a troublemaker. And some of the same people who heard his Gospel will order him to be crucified. They will cheer his persecution. They will put him to death. And afterwards, some will say he deserved it, even the mutilation. The Roman government will consider it "good riddance." If only he had been a good priest, a good nun.

If only he hadn't gotten involved with the poor, the sick, the lame, the blind, the lepers, the unwanted. If only he would have played the game.

Thank God the story doesn't end on the day the God-man on a mule came into Jerusalem. It begins on a mule, it climaxes on the cross. It will end at the empty tomb.

San Isidro, Nicaragua: 1981

IT had all the festive atmosphere of a down-home country picnic in a midwestern rural parish, with one difference. The campesinos of this rural community at the edge of Managua, capital of Nicaragua, were coming together to celebrate death. A new cemetery was being opened this Sunday in a rural community of 570 families of some 3,500 people, and a new potable water system and electrification were being launched, which would bring water and electricity to 300 of the families.

A beautiful makeshift altar had been decorated on this empty cemetery field, which had been donated by the Sandinista government. A local marimba band was providing the music, as campesinos came walking from the hills in all directions to take part.

We were greeted by Padre Rafael Fabretto, a Italian missioner who has been working for thirty years among the Nicaraguan orphans. They tell how he was paralyzed for eight months, had a miraculous cure, and is back with his orphans with a slight limp. Some four kilometers up the road his orphans live in makeshift cabins, donated in 1973 after an earthquake leveled part of Managua. When his orphanage was destroyed in Managua, Father Fabretto gathered up his boys and moved out into this rural community.

The new well and electric pumping station will be located on his grounds, and now the orphans and the surrounding community will have water and light for the first time. The boys still must walk four kilometers back and forth to school each day.

Father Fabretto drove two hundred kilometers today to celebrate Mass and bless the cemetery. He has three orphanages now and lives at one with eighty boys near the Honduran border. He keeps in touch with his boys in the other homes by car and short-wave radio.

During the revolution, which toppled the Somoza government in 1979, Father Fabretto took some of his boys across the Honduran border to a refugee camp.

Manuelo Orazco is in charge of the orphanage at San Isidro. An orphan himself, he is twenty-six years old and now a powerful community leader. He spent three years in a seminary, but now is back with the orphans. For fifteen years he has been part of Father Fabretto's orphanage. "I was one of the problem boys," he says but not now. He is involved in community redevelopment in his district. He is a leader.

Father Fabretto invited me to concelebrate Mass. Manuelo addressed the gathered campesinos, urging them to get involved in community development. Because the government is poor, the people will donate their labor to bring water and light to the area. The government will provide technical assistance, and Catholic Relief Services will put up money for materials.

Both Father Fabretto and Manuelo spoke at Mass of the new cemetery, a symbol of new life in the community, only now no more killings, massacres, and mutilations of the body by government troops. Today they are gathered to celebrate the sacrament of the body, even in death.

After Mass we sit in a wide circle as honored guests in a field nearby, as the orphan boys perform with song and dance. A large piñata, colorfully decorated, hangs overhead, and the festivities are concluded as the boys one by one, blindfolded, try to break the piñata to release candy for all the children.

We walk in solemn procession to the cemetery plot, where two bodies are already buried, to bless the graves and the cemetery.

A young family invites us to a lunch at their simple home — a full-course, typical Nicaraguan Sunday dinner. The orphans follow their beloved padre — he is a sign of hope in their lives — and everyone is fed. One day these boys, like their predecessors, will go on to college and technical schools and become leaders like Manuelo. Father Fabretto, who knows each like a father, will see to that.

The day is capped with a visit to the orphanage, even a baseball game. We see the boys' cabins and their garden, where they raise their own vegetables. It has become an instant love affair for us, but now it is time to go back to Managua. A beautiful, exciting, memorable experience in a campesino barrio comes to an end too quickly. Father Fabretto will drive back to his other orphanage, and Manuelo will take care of his boys and continue to lead the community. A ray of light has broken through in Managua.

Esteli, Nicaragua: 1982

THE women of Esteli, in this northern region of Nicaragua, do not want war. The lines of suffering and oppression are still written on their faces — these mothers and grandmothers with whom we met in a corner of their new but still unfinished Our Lady of Guadalupe church.

Esteli suffered heavy bombing and loss of life during the Sandinista revolution which overthrew the fifty-year dynasty of the Somoza family in July 1979. The bombed out buildings are still in stark evidence in this city which lost two thousand lives in a war to liberate Nicaragua from a one-family dictatorship that left the tiny nation bankrupt and with fifty thousand dead.

This is cattle and coffee country, ninety percent mountainous terrain, reaching some ninety kilometers up to the Honduran border. But it's also subsistent farming area, with employment available only three months a year.

The rugged mountainous area was the place where Somoza recruited and trained his feared national Guardia. Yet it is also where Augusto César Sandino, the hero who inspired the Sandinista revolution, came from. Sandinismo is traditionally strong here, with its origins as a revolutionary movement in 1959.

There is fear of war once again in the faces of the women of Esteli. The ex-Somoza Guardia are organizing again along the Honduran border — some six thousand trained Somocistas — and making counterrevolutionary raids into Nicaragua, with the support of the Honduran and United States military aid. The atmosphere is tense, as the people fear that the U.S. and Honduras will eventually send troops into Nicaragua.

The people — the popular Sandinista Government of Reconstruction — do not want war, which they feel would be more painful than the revolutionary war from which they are still trying to recover.

The women of Esteli — active community and church pastoral workers — talked freely of the conditions in Nicaragua under Somoza before the revolution. Before, they were afraid to go out at night, even to church, but now they can stay out all night and not worry that their family members will not come home safe. Before, they were nobodies because they couldn't read or write and had no dignity as workers and persons. Now, thanks to the literacy campaign of the government, which has lowered the illiteracy rate from fifty percent (one of the highest in Latin America) to twelve percent (the lowest), these women now are at third-grade level of literacy.

One by one they told their personal stories of the revolution. A mother told about her young son, who before he died wrote on the wall in his own blood his faith in the revolution and his Christian faith. An eighty-seven-year-old grandmother, who has seen it all, quoted *Comandante* Tomás Borge: "Christians are part of this revolution because Christians made this revolution." Another woman told how her son went to attend a demonstration and was killed.

A courageous and very forceful mother recalled how the soldiers came to her house, where she was keeping refugees, ordered them all to get in line, and announced they were going to be shot. She refused to get in line, threw herself in front of her husband, whom a soldier had by the throat, to protect him, and began shouting that her husband was a good man. She refused to get in line until finally someone appeared and told the soldiers to let them alone. She could laugh about it now.

But the most poignant story of all came from the lips of a mother who lost seventeen members of her family in the revolution. "Before the revolution," she said, "I was nothing. I was illiterate and had no dignity." Now, thanks to the literacy campaign, she can read and write and take part in community affairs. "Each time I take pen in hand," she said, with tears in her eyes, "I feel I am writing with the blood of my family." We cried with her. The price of human dignity and freedom.

The women of Esteli don't want war. They don't want to lose what they fought for in the revolution. They paid too heavy a price.

Postscript on Esteli: 1983

A YEAR ago I visited Nicaragua as a member of a task force looking into Church-State relations. Our group consisted of three priests and two religious sisters sponsored by CONFER, a confederation of missionary priests and religious working among the poor in Nicaragua. We met with scores of Church leaders, government officials, catechists, delegates of the Word, and Cursillistas to try to sort out what was happening in Nicaragua.

One memorable evening was spent in Esteli at the home of Felipe and Mary Barreda, a dynamic Christian couple active in the Cursillo movement and in the Sandinista revolution. Some twenty priests, religious, lay leaders, and government officials gathered in their home to give us a briefing. We were served an authentic Nicaraguan dinner. The Christian hospitality and warmth of the Barreda family lingers as an unforgettable experience.

I recall this now because I have received word that Felipe and Mary were killed in early April by Contras near the Honduran border. The couple had been kidnapped on December 28, 1982, from a coffee farm in Nicaragua near the border, but word of their murder did not arrive until July 16 when the government made its announcement.

On July 30, five thousand people filled the cathedral in Esteli for a memorial Mass. Upon hearing the news, diocesan officials published a letter in which they recognized the couple's "exemplary, unselfish, tireless, and committed work" in many tasks of the Church's mission. In the letter, the diocese viewed with concern the imminence of an armed conflict and condemned the current political, economic, and military destabilization. The diocese asked the faithful to work hard for peace in a country "which represents a great hope for Christians." The letter was the first time the Catholic hierarchy referred to the suffering being caused by "foreign forces."

Felipe, fifty-two years old, was a native of Esteli. Mary moved there thirty-one years ago when they were married. They had six children and fifteen grandchildren. They were well-off — Felipe a prominent watchmaker and Mary a hairdresser. Traditional Catholics until 1968, they became involved with the Cursillo movement, which convinced them that Christianity should be lived in service to others.

The Barredas were leaders in the diocesan pastoral council, putting into practice their option for the poor by doing social work in marginalized rural areas.

In December 1982, there was a great shortage of coffee-pickers because many were afraid to go to work in areas near the border, due to constant attacks by the Contras. The Nicaraguan government called for volunteers to make sure the annual goal of seventy million tons of coffee was met.

Felipe and Mary were among three thousand volunteers who went from Esteli. On December 23 they and seventy others arrived at Agronica coffee farm, between San Fernando and Jalapa, two kilometers from the Honduran border. On December 28, the farm was surrounded by Contras and besieged with 81mm mortars. Attackers destroyed the harvested coffee and part of the processing machinery and raided the farm house. They kidnapped six pickers, two of whom were the Barredas. Fifty-six others from the area were kidnapped that day.

Four pickers managed to escape. They revealed at a press conference in Esteli on January 9 that Felipe had been wounded by shrapnel during the attack. Contras repeatedly beat him during the journey and threatened to mass-rape Mary. They were taken to a camp in Honduras called La Ladosa. For three days they were bound naked to a tree.

According to military intelligence sources in Nicaragua, the Barredas were killed by the Contras at the beginning of April and buried at the edge of La Ladosa camp.

In a farewell note to friends before leaving Esteli, Mary had written. "The little coffee I'll be able to pick will be converted into health-care facilities, clothing, housing, and roads."

El Salvador: 1984

IN the past four years I have visited Central America five times, but this is my first visit to El Salvador. I undertook this assignment with some little fear and trepidation, because this tiny republic is torn asunder by a senseless war between a military-dominated government and a leftist guerrilla insurgency. The people seem fed up with both. Some sixty thousand have died in the past five years, and over a million have been displaced.

Our plane landed at the airport forty kilometers outside the capital city of San Salvador, and we went immediately by car to the port city of La Libertad to visit the parish of the Immaculate Conception, which is under the pastoral care of two American priests and two laywomen from Cleveland, Ohio. It is one of the three missions sponsored by the Cleveland Diocese in El Salvador, a remarkable twenty-year commitment of resources and personnel to this poverty-stricken, war-torn country of five million people.

It is the same parish where Sister Dorothy Kazel and a lay missioner, Jean Donovan, both from Cleveland, worked before they were raped and murdered, along with two Maryknoll sisters, by the military on December 2, 1980. Their deaths are still being investigated, with little consolation. It was a prayerful beginning to our visit.

Another reflective moment came when we visited the tomb of Archbishop Oscar Romero, also murdered in 1979, because he was outspoken against the oppression being inflicted upon his people.

Archbishop Romero — an uncanonized saint of the poor throughout Central America — is buried in the Cathedral of San Salvador, the scene of violence the day he was buried. His picture can be found everywhere in Central America, especially on the doors of the displaced people, orphanages, diocesan offices, cooperatives, and other social institutions. His name is in graffiti on buildings and walls wherever there is concern for the poor.

His blood, with the blood of four dedicated women and of countless priests, sisters, delegates of the Word, catechists, and members of Christian base communities, has watered the faith of Central America, and one day it will bear fruit in peace and justice.

One elderly campesino I met in an abandoned, unfinished church of San Roque in San Salvador, where three hundred displaced persons have literally been held prisoner for four years, summed it up for me. I had asked him why the military were afraid of him: "What was your crime?" He said, "I believe in God."

It was his belief in God that gave him a thirst for social justice, and now he and his companions are marked people, suspect by the government. In their local rural areas, from which they have fled, they had committed the unpardonable crime of trying to live according to the Gospel. Thankfully, the Church is now protecting them and looking after them at San Roque.

It is a suffering Church in El Salvador, and that is why the Church in North America must come to its aid. The Salvadorans are our brothers and sisters in Christ. Their suffering must become our suffering, their martyrdom ours. Archbishop Arturo Rivera y Damas, the archbishop of San Salvador who succeeded the assassinated Archbishop Romero, is now a lonely voice speaking against the oppression of his people. And his life, too, has been threatened because of his outspoken condemnation of the violation of human rights.

Jesus of Guatemala: 1986

WE were in the highlands of Guatemala, an area of civil unrest, until a year or so ago, marked by constant military incursions to put down peasants suspected of social reform in this violence-torn but beautiful and verdant country often referred to as a country of "the eternal spring."

Now that the civil unrest has somewhat subsided under the democratic civilian government of Vinicio Cerezo, people are free to move about again. In the province of Quichie, the site of so much violence and killings, especially of Church people, the Catholic Church and its bishop had been exiled. Now the province is gradually opening up again to missionary efforts on the part of the Church.

In the wake of the violence and military rule of the early 1980s, the highlands of Guatemala numbers two hundred thousand widows and orphans. Most of the men were killed by the military incursions.

I think I understand now for the first time why the Gospels reflect Jesus' constant concern for widows and orphans. Widows and orphans are the by-products of war, violence, and the displacement of people, something that Old Testament times knew well, as Latin American countries know now.

We were in the highlands to visit projects funded by Catholic Relief Services to meet the employment needs of widows and orphans. The projects abound in the highlands.

This particular evening, after taking part in the opening of a potable water project funded by Catholic Relief Services, we were on our way to the town of Chichicastenango, a popular tourist place until the civil unrest, known for its beautiful church of Santo Tomás and the surrounding marketplace.

It was the Feast of the Triumph of the Cross this particular Sunday when we attended Mass at Santo Tomás, a feast celebrated with great solemnity, followed by a procession through the market area of men carrying a huge cross and a statue of St. Thomas, men and women in colorful native dress, a marimba band, and a long procession of people, amid clouds of incense.

This particular Sunday, during the celebration of Mass, with the women especially dressed for the liturgy, a wedding after the homily, and a funeral after the Mass also took place.

During our time spent in this remarkable handicraft marketplace, suddenly out of nowhere a peasant appeared with a large wooden figure of Jesus on the cross. It was hand-carved, obviously very old, tattered, and worn with dirt and age, but he offered it to me for five dollars, so I clutched it, not knowing how I would get it home, for it was two feet in length, but I was immediately drawn to this Suffering Servant figure of Jesus.

I called to mind the words of Isaiah about the despicable, suffering, almost emaciated figure of Jesus who bears the sins of the world in his body. Indeed, I could count all his ribs in this ancient wood carving, and I thought of the suffering widows and orphans of Guatemala — the sins of poverty and oppression for which my carving of Jesus seemed to be weighed down with and dying. Poverty indeed has been described in these countries of the Third World as slow, agonizing death, and it is.

This Suffering Servant on the Cross became my constant companion through the rest of the trip through Guatemala, then El Salvador and Mexico, as I carried it in my arms over rough and dirty roads, hopeful that he would not be bruised anymore.

I grew close to this Jesus of Guatemala as I carried him safely back to the United States with me, where he shall forever remind me of the widows and orphans of Guatemala, El Salvador, and Mexico.

A Ray of Hope in Guatemala: 1986

IN four villages surrounding the city of Patzun in the department of Chimaltenango, there is a ray of hope for the widows of Guatemala. They are being organized in projects which will provide employment and income.

Taking 35 piglets to market, or raising 125 chickens may not look like the road to economic independence, but for the widows in the Patzun area it is a first step.

The goal of these projects now being developed in the villages around Patzun is to provide agricultural projects to meet the basic needs of the poorest of some 650 families in the area, of whom 100 are headed by widows. There are 35 widows in the village of Chipiacul alone.

We gathered the widows in the churchyard of San Marcos church in the village this Sunday afternoon. What was scheduled as a festive celebration of our visit soon became mingled with tearful moments of remembering. Dozens of widows and children had gathered to welcome us and express their appreciation for the projects for widows funded by Catholic Relief Services. The women prepared a beautiful lunch of chicken and rice and displayed their weaving.

But the memories would not fade away. It was in this very same churchyard that almost forty men were massacred on April 25, 1982, as their frightened families looked on. The two massacres are etched in the memories of widows and children. In the first, twenty men were killed inside the church while they were holding a weekly meeting. In the second, another fourteen were lined up against the outside wall in the back of the church and shot. Their bodies were burned.

It was the feast of St. Mark, the patron of the church, and a Mass and celebration had been held earlier in the afternoon. Come evening, the military moved in and killed the men suspected of being subversives. Whether they were insurgents or not, the story has never been told. Patzun was one of the most violence-torn areas in the early 1980s.

Indigenous Indians constitute half the population of

Guatemala. The other half is mixed. Descended from the Mayan Indians, there are now five major tribes in Guatemala — Quiche, Cachiquel, Tzuthihil, Mam, and Kekchi. While the Indians want to take part in the broad political and economic life of Guatemala and consider themselves Guatemalan, they still have strong ties to their Indian tribes and culture.

Seeds of social and economic unrest have traditionally been sown in the highlands populated by the Indians, and violence has been endemic to the area.

Observers say violence is a way of life throughout Guatemala, and even more so in Guatemala City, which is infested with crime, poverty, arms, and family feuds. They also say that until the rule of law gains respect in Guatemala (a new experience now), the violence will continue.

Despite the violence, the Catholic Church remains committed to social reform and development. The Church will go forward, Archbishop Prospero Pinados reassures his people.

Under the democratic government of Cerezo this past year, much of the tension between the Catholic Church and the government has dissipated. The Church suffered during the early 1980s. Property was seized, and personnel were killed or harassed. It was near persecution. But now relations seem normal again.

Land reform is almost a forbidden subject, even under the civilian government. In the highlands, the land has been subdivided and subdivided until the parcels of land are no longer sufficient to support a family. Along the coast large landholders, many with military alliances, control the large farms, which raise cash crops of cotton and coffee and cattle. Migrant workers drift down that way to work at below-minimum wages.

But the Indians are growing restless. Land reform remains a basic economic issue. In 1980-82, half the population received nineteen percent of the national income, whereas the top quarter received sixty-one percent. The land-poor and the landless are forced into seasonal migrant work, home handicrafts, street vending, and service jobs. Only a quarter of the population has salaried employment.

Guatemala today remains a backward country on the edge of disaster.

My Mexican Friend Juanita: 1986

ON this particular afternoon late in December in Mexico City, I was visiting a newly-formed cooperative for seamstresses who had lost their jobs as a result of the September 19 earthquake that struck Mexico City.

Forty-seven women had joined together from three destroyed garment factories, where another forty-five had lost their lives, mostly single women with children. They had been working in sweatshop conditions.

Thanks to the Archdiocese of Mexico City and Catholic Relief Services, the women were back to work, and as soon as more sewing machines arrive, will be making women's apparel again and will expand their facility to employ 118 women.

Right now they have set up production in a convent and are busy hand-making dolls for temporary income. When I visited them, they were concerned about the future of the doll market now that Christmas had passed.

Then a little light bulb turned on in my head. Why not keep the doll production going by incorporating the dolls into a fundraising drive in the U.S. for their cooperative and for others like them?

And so, Juanita was born, a Mexican doll sent to the U.S. to raise money for seamstresses in Mexico City. Very simply, the idea was to mount a Lenten campaign to raise money for Mexico by offering a free doll (Juanita) for every donation of twenty-five dollars or more to the cooperative movement among seamstresses.

The women were delighted. Depending on the success of the campaign, they could continue to make dolls until they are ready for full garment production. That means sewing machines.

Frankly, I am very excited about the project. I see all kinds of ways to promote Juanita — in parishes by parish organizations taking on a doll project for Lent, or in Catholic schools or by student organizations. I can see priests taking Juanita into the pulpit to preach on Mexican aid. If we could move 3,000 dolls, we could raise $40,000 for the garment workers cooperative in Mexico City.

I can visualize grandparents making a very special gift of Juanita to their grandchildren to teach them about the needs of the poor, or parents, godparents, uncles, and aunts doing the same. Juanita brings the plight of the needy into the home in a very visible, caring way. Juanita speaks for the single mothers, the orphans, the elderly, the unemployed, the homeless of Mexico. She speaks for all Mexican families shattered by the earthquakes.

A Letter from Juanita: 1986

Dear Padre Vicente,

I thought I would write you a few lines to tell you what I have been up to the past few weeks. I want to thank you and Catholic Relief Services for sending me on a personal appearance tour in Phoenix, Denver, Philadelphia, Washington, D.C., Corpus Christi, and even Boise, Idaho, during the month of June.

Your little Mexican doll received a wonderful reception in all these cities, and I understand you have been receiving a good response from my appeal.

Last week, I talked with my godmother, Victoria, who heads up the cooperative 19 de Septiembre in Mexico City. She and the seamstresses who have been hand-making Juanita dolls are so pleased with the response. She tells you have sent $40,000 to Catholic Relief Services and soon will be sending another check. She said she sent you 1,500 more Juanita dolls recently to back up my personal appearance tour.

Victoria said the women are now making dresses and a line of woman's clothes, so they have come a long way since you first proposed they make little Juanitas for the United States to raise money for their cooperative. They want to send you another 5,000 dolls, but I said to hold off awhile to see how the summer goes.

Padre Vicente, the people in the United States are so

wonderful and generous. They have taken me into their families, but most of all into their hearts. One lady wants to sell Juanita dolls in the back of her church, she is so pleased with the effort. Another priest took me into the pulpit and preached about the Mexican earthquake relief — my first time in a pulpit. Padre Vicente, I want to thank you for bringing me to the United States to plead for my suffering people in Mexico who lost their jobs in the earthquake.

As Mr. Lawrence Pezzullo, Executive Director of the CRS wrote to you in June, when you sent CRS $40,000, "The Juanita Project has become an innovative success. I think the real benefit of the program does not lie in the funds raised or the list of names generated, but in the sustained awareness generated by the project. As the TV screen flips from event to event, disaster to disaster, all given equal priority, viewers become somewhat numb. You have developed a way to personalize the contact people have with those affected by tragedy."

Keep me busy, Padre Vicente.

Your loving daughter, Juanita

A Letter from Ghana and Ethiopia: 1983

FROM Vincent, a servant of Christ Jesus and a brother priest called to preach his Good News.

May God our Father and Our Lord Jesus Christ give you grace and peace.

First, I thank God, through Jesus Christ, for all of you because the whole world is hearing of your faith.

I have an obligation to all peoples, to the civilized and to the savage, to the educated and to the ignorant.

I write to you from Africa on behalf of myself and my companions, from this drought-stricken continent where twenty-two nations are facing a catastrophic food shortage. Our sister Beth Griffin from Catholic Relief Services, New York, and our brother John Zierten, photographer, send their greetings.

I ask you to hear them as you hear me because we have

suffered long journeys together for the sake of the Gospel. Twice we have visited Africa, three times Central America, three times Poland, once Lebanon, and once the Far East where we have visited refugees from Cambodia and Laos in Thailand.

We want to remind you, brothers and sisters, of the trouble we had in Ghana and Ethiopia. We felt the sentence of death had been pressed against us, but this happened so that we should rely not on ourselves, but only on God, who raises the dead.

I make an appeal to you to send a brother priest to Ghana to assist in the mission of our brother Andrew, who is all alone as a pastor of a 2,000-family, poverty-ridden inner-city parish embracing 100,000 people in Accra, the capital of Ghana.

Andrew now uses a charcoal stove to cook on, because there is no gas. One week he has gas, next week no water, the following week no electricity, and he doesn't know where to buy sugar and milk.

Our brother, Bishop Dominick Andoh, sends his greetings from Accra and the prayers of the fast-growing churches in Ghana, which now boast twelve percent Catholics of a population of twelve million. Bishop Andoh offered us hospitality. "We don't have much, but what we have we give generously," he said. He speaks warmly of his people despite their terrible hardships.

Even after we arrived in Ethiopia, after a long journey from the west coast of Africa to the east coast, we did not have any rest. There were troubles everywhere, quarrels with government officials, fears in our hearts. We were facing a hostile Marxist government, which had overthrown Emperor Haile Selassie in 1974.

Furthermore, our hearts did ache at the sight of seven million people in the North being severely affected by drought and civil war in the region of Eritrea, Tigre, Gonder, and Wollo.

We want you to know what God's grace has done in the churches of Ethiopia. They are being severely tested by the current troubles, but their joy and generosity is great.

And so are you rich in all you have: in faith, speech, and knowledge, in your eagerness to help. We want you to be generous. For you know the grace of Our Lord Jesus Christ. Rich as he was, he made himself poor for your sake, in order to make you rich by means of his poverty.

I am not trying to relieve others by putting a burden on you; but since you have plenty at this time, it is only fair that you should help those who are in need.

And now, my brothers and sisters, good-bye. I long to visit you. Strive for perfection; listen to my appeals; agree with one another, and live in peace. And the God of love and peace be with you.

All God's people in Ghana and Ethiopia send you their greetings.

Warsaw, Poland: 1981

THE clickety-clack sounds of a European train rumbling through the countryside of Poland between Katowice and Warsaw provided the setting for a reflection on Poland this late September evening. It was the last leg of a too-short five-day trip to Poland.

The night air freshened my face as I stood in the aisle outside our compartment before an open window.

Unlike the train from Munich to Geneva we'd taken a week earlier, this Polish train had no diner, or should I say, a diner with nothing to offer but a few pieces of bread and hot tea or a bottle of lemon drink. The diner was symbolic of the food shortages we were to encounter throughout our stay in Poland — long lines of people waiting to get a weekly ration of meat or bread or milk or whatever. One line in Katowice was more than a block long, three abreast, as people queued up to get toothpaste.

The night before in Germany as we were to leave for Berlin, Beth Griffin, of Catholic Relief Services in New York City, called to inquire whether photographer John Zierten and I would join her in a five-day trip to Poland at the end of our German trip.

The only problem was whether John and I could get visas. On September 25, visas in hand, we flew from Geneva to Warsaw. After following the CRS operation in Warsaw on September 26, we took a night train to Gdansk. Things began to happen in

Gdansk, the shipping port of Poland along the Baltic sea, the historic city where World War II began when 187 valiant Polish soldiers battled 6,000 German troops. Gdansk is also the city where Solidarity was founded a year ago when the shipyard workers pulled off a general strike and Lech Walesa emerged as the charismatic leader of Solidarity.

Solidarity has profoundly shaken the Communist foundations of Poland and in effect has shattered Poland's links with the Soviet Union.

When we visited Father Henry Jankowski, the unofficial chaplain to Solidarity, he arranged for us to attend the Solidarity Congress in the vast sports arena where nine hundred delegates were attending their first national congress.

We received a warm reception at the Congress and met Lech Walesa, a very strong Catholic and a daily communicant, who attended the opening Mass I was privileged to concelebrate with the pastor of the Gdansk cathedral and Father Joseph Tischner from Krakow, a leading intellectual in the Church. The Mass at this historic occasion was the highlight of my visit to Poland.

It was a week of tension in Poland, as Solidarity, a free labor union of ten million workers, was observing the first anniversary of the general strikes that started a year ago last August in the Gdansk shipyards, giving birth to Solidarity and projecting its leader, Lech Walesa, on the international scene as one of Poland's strongest national figures.

My quick first impressions of the Catholic Church which has given us our first Polish Pope, John Paul II, is that the Church is very strong and powerful, but also very macho. The faith and courage of the Polish people, a high percentage of them practicing Catholics (thirty-six million Catholics out of a population of thirty-eight million), is almost unbelievable in our Western world today.

At a time when the Church seems on the decline in the West, it is strong and growing in Poland, and this fact alone gives an insight into the source of the powerful male leadership of John Paul II.

Because of its thirty-five-year confrontation with the

Communist state, the Church in Poland stands tall. It has unified the people, especially now in this time of economic strain.

To be honest, the Catholic Church in Poland, because of its strong position in a Communist country, has yet to undergo a kind of reform the Church in Western countries and the United States has undergone in the Vatican II conciliar age. It has its hands full contending with Communism.

If there are stirrings for renewal in the Polish Church, they have been subordinated to the greater good of unity vis à vis the Polish government.

So for me to visit the Catholic Church in Poland — its rectories, convents, chancery offices — and to meet with Polish bishops, priests, and religious sisters as we did is to step back into the 1950s in the United States. It is to be in contact with a church overflowing with priests, sisters, and vocations.

It is a church that still has no need for a multiplication of lay ministries as we have experienced it, when priests are plentiful, they seem to say.

It is a church that has strong clerical leadership, with religious sisters in the background. Yet with all of this kind of clericalism, it is a church that is very close to the people, very sacramental, very respected and loved by the people.

The phenomenon of full churches on Sundays, with strong male attendance, good liturgies, but always centered on the Mass, good singing — all this is praiseworthy.

One of the highlights of the trip was the opportunity to concelebrate a Mass opening one of the sessions of the Solidarity Congress in Gdansk. Each day the Congress opened with a Mass, as these hardy workers, predominantly male, attended Mass and received Communion, and lined up on the Congress floor for confession.

It was an unforgettable experience.

We stayed at convents on our trip — full convents of traditional Polish nuns. They were a happy, joyful lot, of all ages, and we enjoyed their hospitality no end.

There was no talk of optional celibacy or of ordaining women priests.

So the lasting impression from all of this is that the Church — as well as the Faith — is alive and well in Poland.

One thing is certain, there is a great diversity of culture between Poland and West Germany, or the United States. The Catholic Church of Poland has taken on its own unique character. We need to appreciate the difference.

The Pilgrim Pope in Poland: 1983

WITHOUT a doubt, Pope John Paul II has emerged as the most powerful leader in the world today by the sheer force of his personality and the spiritual message of the teachings of Jesus Christ that he proclaims during his world travels as Vicar of Christ.

Never was this more evident than during his June 1983 visit to his native Poland, where an estimated fifteen million Poles came from all over Poland to be near him, to pray with him, and to place their hopes in him. All of this is more remarkable considering it took place in a Communist nation behind the Iron Curtain and under a military regime and the restrictions of martial law.

The outpouring of the Polish people to join their spiritual leader on his pilgrimage to Jasna Gora monastery in Czestochowa was a powerful witness to the religious faith of the people in spite of sufferings recently experienced at the hands of the government. The trip was the fulfillment of a promise the Holy Father made in 1979 when he first visited Poland under more festive circumstances.

Solidarity, a mass movement of ten million workers, flourished at the first papal visit. Under the leadership of Lech Walesa, Solidarity brought a breath of freedom to Poland and reached a climax with its first national congress in 1981.

Then came the ultimate humiliation. Solidarity was banned and outlawed, and martial law was imposed on the long-suffering nation in December 1981, amid severe economic depression marked by shortages of consumer goods and long lines of people under rationing.

To the credit of the government of prime minister General Wojciech Jaruzelski, Poland honored its invitation to the Holy Father for his return to Poland to celebrate the Jasna Gora anniversary. How the gamble will eventually pay off awaits future events in Poland and the Soviet Union.

But return the Pope did June 16-23 for a spiritual pilgrimage to the Marian shrines in Warsaw, Poznan, Czestochowa, Katowice, Wroclaw, Nowa Huta, and Krakow. By their outpouring, the Polish people quietly and reverently demonstrated their faith and their support for the spirit of freedom, democracy, and workers' rights that Solidarity had unleashed in their midst.

In apocalyptic terms, the Holy Father was looking to the future of Poland, indeed of all Eastern Europe, toward the third millennium, rather than to quick or transitory fixes in the social life of the people. "Christ the same yesterday, today, and forever," he said in an outdoor Mass in Warsaw, where he set the tone and the mood of his visit.

The history of Poland indeed has been tied up with Jesus Christ for a thousand years, and for six centuries with the Mother of Christ under the figure of the Black Madonna. The broad outlines of the Pope's message took into consideration Poland's rights of sovereignty; a yearning for a new victory, won through effort and the Cross and achieved through defeats; civic and workers' rights, to be achieved through dialogue between those who govern and those who are governed.

Through the eyes of John Paul II, the history and culture of Poland are intermingled with the religious traditions of the country — its saints, its *beati*, its shrines to the Mother of Poland, and more recent heroes such as Saint Maximilian Kolbe and the late Cardinal Stefan Wyszynski.

In perhaps his most moving and poignant address, at Jasna Gora monastery "in an hour of frankness," Pope John Paul II opened his heart as he appealed to Our Lady of Jasna Gora to stand by those who are suffering. He entrusted Poland to her.

"I am a son of that nation; therefore, I deeply feel its noble aspirations — the wish to love in truth, liberty, and justice, social solidarity, the wish to love one's own life. I wish to entrust to our

Mother of Jasna Gora all that has been worked out in difficult times of the past few years, particularly since August [The Gdansk agreements].

"Finally, Our Lady of Jasna Gora, I have come here to tell you once again '*totus tuus*.' O Mother, I am all yours, and all that is mine is yours. All that is mine, that means also my homeland, my nation. O Mother, I have been called to the service of the universal Church of Peter. With a mind to the universal service I constantly repeat '*totus tuus*.' I wish to be a servant to all and at the same time I am the son of this land, this nation. This is my people, my home, and, Mother, all that is mine is yours."

It would be untrue to the Holy Father's message to expect dramatic changes in Poland immediately, but without a doubt, his words in due time will have a cataclysmic effect throughout all of Eastern Europe. Short-term results are transitory, but a moral and spiritual renewal of Poland — and Eastern Europe — could revive the Church around the world.

The peacefulness of the immense crowds of pilgrims was most impressive. Even the Solidarity demonstrations, unplanned, were orderly if spirited and did not require police actions. There was plenty of military presence at all events. The people used the Solidarity gesture of two raised fingers everywhere to express their feelings.

As usual, many walked for miles to be with the Pope. We would see entire parish delegations, led by the priests, carrying a crucifix and parish banners, walking the roads late at night toward the pilgrimage sites, as we traveled by bus from site to site.

The countryside was full of pilgrims. They carried food in shopping bags day and night, and once they arrived they would stand for hours packed together in human solidarity, waiting for the Holy Father. They sang and they prayed in anticipation, then remained for the concelebrated Mass and the homily of the Pope.

It is almost an indescribable witness of religious faith amid all kinds of hardships and sufferings. Something is happening in Poland — and the Holy Father senses it — that might someday renew the Church in Eastern Europe, and perhaps eventually even the West.

The turnout of the people, an estimated sixteen million, in a country behind the Iron Curtain still under restrictions of a military regime, surely makes the recent visit of the Pope to Poland the most remarkable news event of 1983. I am glad we were there.

Lebanon in Turmoil: 1983-85

GETTING *in* is never a problem, but getting *out* is. A recent visit to Lebanon has been no exception to this rule.

On an overnight trip to the North of Lebanon, we visited the war-torn ruins of the port city of Tripoli, which until a few short weeks ago had undergone continuous fighting between pro- and anti-Syrian forces. On a visit to the badly shelled old quarter of Tripoli, a group of young anti-Syrian commandos, armed with Russian-made rifles, took us under their protection for a tour of the ruins. It was a scary few hours, but then no one refuses the hospitality of a dozen teenagers armed to the teeth. Fortunately, they were friendly. We were told later that had a group of pro-Syrian soldiers accosted us, our fate may not have been so pleasant.

Another overnight trip took us east of Beirut up through the hill towns, then down into the fertile Bekaa Valley to the ancient city of Baalbek. This too was Syrian-controlled, once we got to Baalbek. The Syrian soldiers were very friendly with us there, as were the PLO we met in a Palestinian refugee camp in Baalbek.

The next day we started our trek back to Beirut, early enough, because we were told to leave before a huge Iranian festival began in Baalbek in celebration of the fourth anniversary of Khomeini's revolution in Iran. We were told the roads might be closed for the day to celebrate the festivities. We got out early, but heard later that 1,600 Iranians celebrated the day in Baalbek. Americans would not have been honored guests at the festivities.

On the way back to Baalbek, trouble began to haunt us. On our visit to a Jesuit-founded school for Muslim children in the hill town of Ta'atabnaya, which had received construction funds from

Catholic Relief Services to rebuild after shelling in the area late last summer, excitement began. During the summer, troops from Iran, Bangladesh, East Germany, Somalia, and Pakistan had come to help expel the Israelis. Some twelve kilometers away we could hear Syrian artillery and see the smoke rising. It was a routine exchange between the Syrians and the Israelis. We thought it best to keep moving.

All was well until we reached an Israeli military checkpoint at Sofar, where traffic had been stopped because of some trouble in the area. A tire also went flat. After an hour's delay, we persuaded the Israelis to let us through because we were due back in Beirut.

They finally gave us clearance, but from then on through the hill towns to Aley, where the Druzes (an Islamic group) and the Christians had been shooting it out, and almost back to Beirut, we drove through ghost towns.

Not only was ours the only car on the road, but all the shops were closed, homes were shuttered, and not a person was in sight in town after town — the same towns that were bustling with activity the day before when we came up the same road headed for Baalbek.

It was an eerie feeling and scary, as we passed one military lookout after another, as though all was silent before a big storm. Our spare tire went flat along the way, but we finally found a place to have it repaired.

Beirut, as militarized as it is, was a welcome sight when we once arrived back, even though we had our moments in Beirut. On the afternoon we were driving back to Beirut, the Palestinian Research Center some four blocks from our hotel was blown up and a number of people were killed or wounded. Trouble always seemed to be exploding just behind us or in front of us, but that is the shell game most Lebanese live under every day. It is a question of being in the right place at the right time to survive.

Later we went South to Tyre and Sidon, then under Israeli control and protected also by the Christians, and again without incident we passed through garrisoned refugee camps.

Finally, we toured the Sabra and Shatila PLO refugee camps outside Beirut, which had been the scene of an earlier massacre and were a rubble heap, more recently attacked again.

The next day we left Beirut for the United States. Incidentally, in the central hills of Lebanon, which we drove through on our way back from Baalbek, severe blizzards have since stranded hundreds in cars on the roads, and many have died. The blizzards hit several days after we passed through them.

It was the panorama of Lebanon we saw, with some sixteen warring factions, ethnic and religious, some just old-fashioned family feuds, where holding people hostage has been a way of life. There were more guns than people in Lebanon.

Sunday I celebrated Mass for the Marines outside the Beirut airport at a camp to be besieged by terrorists a few months later, where we would lose 241 of our Marines. The group of Marines we spent that Sunday morning with were a happy lot, because they were on their way home, a new group to replace them. It was the new group that suffered the massacre.

Wherever we went we visited orphanages, schools for the blind, the elderly, the handicapped, all of them suffering from the cruelty and dislocations of Lebanon's constant civil turmoil. Sometimes we forget about all those children who suffer from these constant bombardings until we see the deaf, blind, or orphaned children, the crippled, and the handicapped.

Amid all this turmoil, Lebanese life goes on. After a bombing — and there were several in the city while we were there and many since, including the hotel we stayed in — the people crawl out of the wreckage like ants and began immediately to rebuild their buildings, clear the rubble, get the system moving again. The stores reopen and people continue to make do. On and on it goes, but this nation never falters. It just sinks deeper into anarchy and political chaos.

Here is where the seeds of international terrorism are sown. For the Lebanese people terrorism is a way of life — like gangs in the big American cities. For us it is barbarism, uncivilized and shocking.

Lebanon remains a huge Pac-Man screen where all kinds of ethnic, religious, and political groups play out their war games.

The United States should be happy to be out of there.

Mission to Zambia: 1988

Two weeks in an African republic like Zambia, which is a little larger than Texas, is not long enough to get a complete feel for the country, its people, or the life of the Church. Yet I was able to visit three of the four major geographic areas in Zambia, including rural missions, copper-mining towns, and the urban shantytowns and suburban parishes in and around the capital city of Lusaka.

The Catholic missions, staffed in the beginning by foreign missioners, are slowly becoming Africanized as young Zambians are attracted both to the diocesan priesthood and to religious communities. This is even more obvious among religious communities of women. And of course, most lay catechists and lay workers are Zambian.

We can learn much from the missionary approach in Africa. I visited a number of mission compounds that have developed over the past fifty years. They are complex institutions: churches, friaries, schools, hospitals, clinics, house of formation, workshops for training young people in carpentry or sewing, and farms. They are centers of vitality to which people come in need, whether located in a rural bush area or in the center of a shantytown.

Depending on the size of the territory (rural or urban), a mission center may serve up to a hundred thousand people and cover up to a hundred kilometers. Always there are a number of outstations (prayer chapels or centers), anywhere from three to twenty, attached to the mission center.

Each outstation may minister to up to a hundred Christians or more. There is a full-time paid lay catechist from the area and often part-time catechists. The people gather on Sunday (and other days) for prayer, Scripture reading, and discussion of social needs.

Depending on the numbers and size of the mission, a priest may visit a prayer center once a month or four times as year to celebrate the Eucharist. The rest of the time the centers are on their own, complete with parish councils. In other words, the Catholic Church has a substructure of outstations throughout Zambia, which guarantees the presence of the Church and evangelization in the event priests are no longer available.

As a typical American journalist, albeit a priest, I learned a powerful lesson about African values one day visiting a rural outstation. Knowing we were on a crowded schedule, when we entered the village I began taking pictures and getting my tape recorder ready for quick interviews before we moved on to the next station. I was in a hurry to get my stories.

On my way out, one of the lay workers stopped me and was somewhat upset because I hadn't greeted everyone personally before I began my work. Then I realized how much the Africans attach to personal greetings. People come first. Time is secondary. Hospitality is more important than deadlines. Friendship is of first importance.

Time for the African means "today," which permits for healthy relationships. Linked with the cult of friendship is hospitality. Africans are willing to make every sacrifice for a guest.

I came to love my Zambian brothers and sisters as a warmhearted, friendly, and above all, peace-loving people. They made me feel at home.

Father Ronan Herlihy, O.F.M. Cap., a veteran missionary in Zambia from Ireland, told me this story when I visited his mission in the Diocese of Livingstone, in this south-central African republic. A year or so ago he visited the United States to appeal for funds for his mission. He was introduced in one parish in New Jersey as a missionary from Zambia, Central America.

Three months ago I didn't know where Zambia was located myself. I soon found out when I was invited by the apostolic pronuncio for Zambia and Malawi, Archbishop Eugenio Sbarbaro, to write some stories on the Church in Zambia and to act as a consultant to the Zambian Episcopal Conference on Communications.

I told Father Ronan not to be alarmed. Most Americans don't know where Nicaragua is. Zambia is a little-known, developing Third World nation, bordered by eight other African nations. Formerly known as Northern Rhodesia, Zambia achieved independence from Great Britain in 1964. The African name

Zambia is taken from the famous Zambezi river, which flows in and out of Angola and Zambia and empties into the spectacular Victoria Falls near Livingstone at the border of Zimbabwe (Southern Rhodesia) and Zambia.

My trip was completely church-oriented. I stayed in Catholic missions in rural areas, in urban areas, and in the copper belt mining towns. In Livingstone, I was the guest of the Capuchins. In Lusaka, the capital city, I stayed with Archbishop Sbarbaro, but forayed into the neighboring missions where I conducted interviews; in Ndola and Kitwe in the copper belt, I was the guest of the Conventual Franciscans, many of whom are from Italy, and I lived in their missions.

For two weeks I lived life as an African missionary. I lived in the large mission compounds, visited mission projects (schools, hospitals, seminaries, the mission press, special programs for the handicapped, the deaf and dumb, lepers, and secondary schools for girls). I followed the missionaries to their outposts in the deepest bush area.

I talked with African bishops, native priests, and religious sisters, officials of the episcopal conference, missionaries from nineteen countries of the world, seminary rectors, and pastors. It was a full, exciting two weeks. In Zambia I witnessed a vibrant, young African Church at work in a peaceful and tranquil political climate under President Kenneth Kaunda.

In sixty short years, since the foreign missionaries planted permanent roots in Zambia (although the first missionaries date back a hundred years), the Church has grown to nearly thirty percent of the population.

I hope to return to Zambia to spend time in the northern area of the Archdiocese of Kasama (the most Catholic area of Zambia) and the small African nation of Malawi.

PART FOUR:

In the Footsteps of Jesus

I INVITE you to retrace with me a spiritual journey I made alone with Jesus. It was such an exciting and eventful religious experience for me, I feel the need to share at least some of the highlights of it. The goal was to let the Lord speak to me this week and for the Lord to listen to my heart, as though through a stethoscope. It was a closed retreat.

This particular week was to be spent on vacation with the Lord, a real vacation with Jesus, and him only. I was invited to pray over Psalm 139 and Isaiah 43:1-4. What a help this was, because Psalm 139 ended with the plea to the Lord: "Examine me, O God, and know my mind. Test me, and discover my thoughts. Find out if there is any evil in me, and guide me in the everlasting way." The answer to this plea comes through the lips of Isaiah: "Do not be afraid — I am with you. Your troubles will not overcome you."

"I am with you." Finally, I was now at ease with Jesus. He and I would spend the rest of the week together. Our vacation had begun. Jesus and I will surely vacation together this week. There will be times when we will pray together, but also times when we will goof off, relax, enjoy each other's company in a long walk, or sit alone in the great outdoors, or jog around the lake. We will be together in a variety of ways.

But Lord, how do I gain access to your heart, and how will you gain access to mine? That will be our great adventure. How do I discover the heart of Jesus? So many people I am working with, especially young people, want me to show them the heart of Jesus in my relationships with them. What they really want is access to your heart, O Lord, whether they articulate this or not. Help me make your heart my heart, so I can give it to them.

My goal was to select one of the four Gospels to pray over the rest of the week. How did Jesus deal with people, both public and private. I chose the Gospel of Mark. I put myself in the Gospel scenes. Watch and learn how Jesus deals with me. The Jesus of Mark's Gospel became my companion for the week.

Mark is an action Gospel, almost a news-story account of the life of Jesus. Mark could have written for *USA Today*. He gives the facts, he describes the action, and he digests the teaching. No long discourses, as in John. When you are with the Jesus of Mark, you are on the move. I found this very comfortable with my own lifestyle.

I decided to concentrate on those passages that had to do with the relationships of Jesus with his disciples. What was the interaction between Jesus and his disciples?

My first set of readings had to do with how Jesus called his disciples and what their life together must have been like on the dusty roads of Galilee or on the unpredictable waters of Lake Galilee, which is where much of his ministry took place.

I put myself in the scene as Andrew, the very first disciple Jesus called, and I became part of the apostolic team. What did they talk about? Did they sing songs, cook out, fish, play some kinds of stick games, engage in light banter? Did the apostles talk about personal problems, home life, girls?

I, now Andrew, started out as a friend and a follower of Jesus. Jesus, first of all, must become friends with his disciples, then later form them, teach them, and send them out. What kind of friendship? That was my search as I tried to relate all this to my ministry.

So Jesus spends a lot of time with his disciples after calling them. They follow him on long walks from town to town. They spend time with him in a boat sailing back and forth across the lake. They are with him when he drives out demons, cures the sick, when he feeds them on the Sabbath, or calms the waters.

In all of these associations and a variety of experiences, Jesus is building friendship and trust. He defends them against the Pharisees. He sleeps during the storm, then calms the winds and waves. Now the disciples trust him.

That was my first lesson about the heart of Jesus. I, Andrew, was first a friend of Jesus, then a disciple, and finally an apostle.

As I continue my journey with Jesus, I find myself more and more placing myself in the sandals of the disciple Andrew.

Why me, Jesus? I am Andrew. I am a fisherman — young, uneducated, rough and tough, of simple origins. How did I get caught up in your nets? Why me? I didn't know you. I never saw you before. What was the chemistry between us. First, a fascination, because I had heard of John the Baptist. I needed a friend. You were interested in me. I still don't know much about you. I visit your home. You invite me back.

Then I go tell Simon, James, and John, and Nathanael and Philip (my cousins). You meet us at the lake when we were fishing. You tell us to come follow you. We do. Drop everything. Our fishing jobs, our families. Why? We are thrown together.

From now it will be day and night along roads, in towns, on the lake. We go to a wedding feast. You change water into wine. You relate well with people. We meet your mother.

People crowd around you. You cut through the arguments of the Pharisees. You drive out evil spirits, heal the sick, preach in the synagogues, take on lawyers and priests, associate with outcasts. I am part of all this. It is scary.

Then one day you take us aside, twelve of us, and make us a part of your work. You send us out, two by two, to do what you have been doing. We preach, we drive out demons, we heal, we tell people to reform their lives because the kingdom of God is at hand. It all started so simply, but it has gotten heavy.

The day we return from our mission we find Jesus surrounded by crowds. He sees us and invites us to get away with him where we can talk and rest. We have so much to tell him, and he wants to hear all about it. We head across the lake in a boat, but on the other side the crowds have gathered. They had walked around the lake to be there when we arrived. Jesus sees them, and is filled with pity. He begins to teach.

I, Andrew, and the others beg him to send them away early, so they can have time to get some food. Jesus says to us. "No, you feed them." How? We don't have the money. So he takes five loaves of bread and two fishes, blesses them, and feeds five thousand people. We leave immediately by boat, but Jesus says he will catch up with us after he dismisses the crowd. Maybe now we will have some time with him.

Jesus goes into the hills to pray, then he comes looking for us. We are on the stormy water of Lake Galilee. When he sees us, he literally walks on the waters to get to us. We cross the lake with him, and once again a crowd awaits him.

This was an action-packed two days. Everyone wants a piece of Jesus — the crowds and his apostles. Finally, he must get away himself to pray and spend some time with his Father. Jesus comes across as anxious of heart. He wants to be with his disciples, but the crowds keep pulling at him. He is torn between the needs of the people and his love for his twelve apostles. He seems to be in a hurry to satisfy both needs. He wants to get it all done and now, but the Father seems to say to him, "Slow down. Come and pray awhile. You'll get to be with the twelve."

There has to be joy in the heart of Jesus to see the apostles upon their return from the mission. They have so much to share. But the crowds make their demands also, and Jesus shows pity on them, performing the miracle of the loaves and fishes.

Then he spends time with the Father in prayer before rejoining his apostles — so anxious to be with them he simply walked on the waters to catch up with them. What a beautiful gesture of love. Now we have him alone on the lake. Now we can have a few intimate moments together with him. We tell him more of our story and he brings us up to date. But tomorrow is another day. We head to the shore in the morning. The crowds again await Jesus.

But the euphoria would soon come to an end. Along with the high moments of intimacy and friendship with Jesus and being associated with him in his ministry and his teaching, there would be days of testing. I speak as Andrew.

All of this seemed to have a beginning when Jesus first began speaking to us of his approaching death and resurrection. We just didn't understand what he was talking about, or if we did we simply didn't want to hear it, and we became afraid to ask him. Jesus himself seemed to be struggling with the same thoughts. For a moment, he seemed to have an identity crisis when he asked us who we thought he was? When Simon told him he was the Messiah, the Son of God, he seemed overjoyed.

But little things began to irritate us and him. When we argued among ourselves about who will be the greatest in the kingdom, who will be first, Jesus became angry with us. There was jealousy when John saw another, not one of us, driving out demons. Jesus chided him for that.

When he tells the rich young man how difficult it will be for the rich to enter the kingdom, we are shocked. We still have some hopes and visions of getting something out of our friendship with Jesus. What's in it for us? Jesus is again distressed. And later on, when James and John ask whether they can be with Jesus on either side in the kingdom, both Jesus and ourselves are angered, and Jesus lectures us on the cost of discipleship.

If there seem to be tensions among us, it is because it is not the same anymore. Jesus' mind seems elsewhere, he is troubled, and we begin arguing among ourselves.

As we push toward Jerusalem, Jesus continues to draw crowds, but he seems preoccupied. He snaps at us when we keep the children from him. He curses the fig tree, then the moneychangers in the temple area. We never saw that side of his heart before. He is acting as though time is running out, as he tries to handle his approaching death. Then a great calm comes over him, and he teaches us how to pray and seems to ask forgiveness, as if forgiving us for bickering among ourselves, and asking us our forgiveness for his ill mood.

It seems that our relationship with Jesus had to go through a purification at this time. It had been a wonderful, upbeat relationship from the time he called us until he began talking about his approaching death. We could handle the joy, but could we handle this? We had to purify our motives now. It was down to the stark reality of facing life without the presence, support, and love of Jesus.

We had to tighten up our ship, purify our relationship with one another, deal with jealousies and ambitions. We had to get all of this out of our systems and become the "least," the servants of the kingdom. And now we must prepare ourselves for the rest of the drama — the suffering, death, and resurrection of Jesus.

Honestly, I, Andrew, am scared. Can I walk the last mile? Then what? Do I go back to fishing?

What I have learned from the heart of Jesus from these tests is that it can express anger, it can have a short fuse, it can be troubled, preoccupied. It can be scared by suffering and death. It seeks affirmation. It is vulnerable. It is anxious. It is healing, and it can ask for forgiveness.

I am beginning to feel comfortable with the heart of Jesus, as my vacation with Jesus winds down.

After the last meal Jesus ate with his disciples the night before he died, the disciples fade into the background. Jesus himself seems prepared to spend his final hours alone, just he and the Father. The action now centers on Jesus and his ordeal. The disciples gradually will disappear and will not be around at the moment of his death. It is Jesus confronting his death alone.

Jesus doesn't seem overly distraught at the defection of his disciples (apart from John), as though he expected this as part of his ordeal. After all, the final sacrifice is between himself and the Father now. The relationship with the twelve apostles, as they had known it, was now over. It was as if Jesus now felt the need to detach himself from all human relationships. He is face to face with the Father. He is even disinterested in the court proceedings, as events become irreversible.

What about the twelve? Were they as detached as Jesus? Probably not, but it was his death that was unfolding, not theirs. What could they do? Once they saw the beginning of the end — trial, sentence, suffering, death — they bailed out, disappeared into the crowd. Events were beyond their control.

Judas betrays Jesus. Peter wants to be faithful, but even he couldn't face reality. He is frightened, and he doesn't want to be arrested. Three of the disciples couldn't wait and watch as Jesus prayed. They probably didn't understand the importance of the moment.

I am Andrew. How do I feel? Jesus didn't make any great effort to take us with him to the cross. He left us free. He seemed to be saying, "It isn't going to be pretty. I leave you with happier memories of our last meal together. Let's part on that moment of intimacy. After all, I will come back to get you. Meet me in Galilee. It was like he and the Father had this thing between them, and he had to work it out.

How do I feel? I am losing a friend. My life has been different since Jesus first touched me. Since that first calling, I have experienced Jesus a hundred ways. He indeed was a man of God. He taught me how to live, how to love, how to pray, how to teach, how to heal, and now how to suffer and die.

I don't think I could have handled his suffering and death. I think he sensed this. It would have been unbearable to watch and not be able to do anything.

I, Andrew. What next? I hope we see him in Galilee, as he said, because I am depressed now. It is all over, and I feel hanging in midair, with no place to go, nothing to do, no Jesus, no more twelve together like we were. The sheep are scattered. I have to catch up with the others.

Jesus called us his friends. No greater love than he lay down his life for his friends. He died alone, but for us. His death was the greatest sign of friendship he could show us.

Jesus must have thought of me when he died. The twelve must have been in his heart. He had to see the faces of Andrew, Peter, James, John, and the rest during his final moments on the cross.

What did I learn about the heart of Jesus these final days? I, Vincent, am now praying. Well, Jesus could be detached and step back from deep personal relationships.

He could let go. His heart could handle betrayal, denial, unfaithfulness, misunderstanding. He had a heart that always put love of the Father ahead of love for his disciples.

It was a heart that could be weak at times, as in the garden in prayer, where he admits vulnerability. Finally, I discovered a heavy heart as well as a light heart, and a forgiving heart right up to the cross.

At times I have played the role of Andrew, the first apostle. Other times I tried to put myself in the role of Jesus interacting with the twelve, and still other times, I took the role of Vincent in terms of my own priesthood.

The final journey begins with the resurrection of Jesus, and in Marcan style, is terse and brief. The women continue to tend to Jesus as they prepare him for the tomb. But where are the disciples? Are they still frightened, in hiding, afraid of the authorities?

After the resurrection, Jesus catches up with the disciples in Galilee, as he had promised. They didn't believe the first report, and Jesus is angry with them, more because of their lack of faith than anything else. "How do you preach if you don't believe?" he asks them.

Then, to the point. Jesus commissions them to preach the Gospel to everyone and to baptize. Then he leaves them, and the disciples go forth to carry out the mission, with no questions asked.

Again, I am Andrew. What are my feelings? Well, Jesus is all business now. The days of human friendship are finished. His mind is fixed on heaven, but he wants his work on earth continued. We are called to that work and we accept.

Actually, I am relieved. I was afraid it all had ended on the cross. I had concerns about my future. Go back to fishing? Never work with the other disciples again? Were these past several years a nightmare? Did Jesus prepare us for naught? How could he be so cold and indifferent to our needs? But now the excitement is back. He has given us a job to do in his absence. He trusts us. He even puts Peter in charge, and that's good. We need a leader, and Peter can handle it.

Now, Jesus must have looked upon this frail band of disciples whom he loved. They have been through a lot together. They have come this far with Jesus. They are all he has, so they may as well go all the way together. They are human, not God. They are basically good people, despite all their faults and weaknesses.

After all, Jesus chose them, they didn't choose him. Jesus believes in them. He trusts them. He loves them. He'll not leave them orphans. Someday he'll gather them together again and present them as his special gift to the Father. After all, they are part of him and he is a part of them. They are one, and the Father will be pleased.

In a way, Jesus feels compassion for them, because they have no idea what lies ahead, even though he does. Their utter sincerity is going to be rewarded in altogether unexpected ways. What they receive is not what they hoped for when Jesus first met them. And the price they will have to pay — the suffering, rejection, persecution, death — well, it's a good thing they can't see it now.

The rewards? Consolation probably more than anything. A sense of serving Jesus, seeing the Good News preached to the poor, the needy tended to, the word spread, the Christian community taking roots.

Then, the final reward when Jesus and the disciples gather together again for an eternal life of friendship with one another and the Father. Then they will know and love the Father as Jesus did.

Then it will all make sense.

Finally, I, Vincent, thank you, Jesus, for this wonderful vacation together. Just a final request, which I sense you have already granted. Help me to love my disciples as you loved yours.

Paradoxes

A YEAR later my guide is the Gospel of Luke, the compassionate Gospel, in order to discover the compassion of Jesus, so that I might become more compassionate in my own life.

And so some reflections on the Gospel of Luke, disjointed in a way, but as the Holy Spirit moved me. Once again, absolutely no outside interference, no contact with the outside world, no productive work during the week, carried out in solitude and silence. In this perspective, the following paradoxes of the spiritual life came to mind.

Silence and Solitude

SILENCE speaks louder than words.

To be apart from friends is to be closer to them.

To fast is to satisfy a deeper hunger.

Quiet can be deafening. Crickets sound like bulldozers.

To be alone is to be with the Other. To be lonely is to be apart from the Other.

Aloneness is togetherness.

Prayer is aloneness with God; loneliness, without God.

Solitude is a state of mind. I can experience solitude on a busy street corner, when with a friend or in a family, either in a traffic jam or walking through a forest.

Solitude is an ambience created by the mind, desired by the heart, willed by the spirit.

Solitude is a good.

Silence is a good.

Aloneness is a good.

Loneliness is a good.

Fasting is a good.

Prayer is a good.

A retreat that combines all of the above is a good retreat.

Jesus experienced solitude, quiet, silence, aloneness, loneliness, fasting, and prayer as he hung on the cross. The cross was his retreat.

Jesus suffered and died alone. All was quiet within.

He was alone and lonely. He was thirsty, and he cried out only in prayer to the Father.

All was consummated. All was finished. Jesus died alone.

Each of us must one day die alone. Death is quiet, lonely, silent.

A retreat is like death. It is silent, quiet, prayerful, alone, empty, lonely.

A retreat is a foretaste of death and resurrection, a sign of new life to come. A retreat is Advent and Christmas (becoming and being), Good Friday and Easter (letting go and becoming new), in that order.

Anticipation, birth, dying, and rebirth. The story of life.

Passion and Compassion

IN the Gospel of St. Luke we read these words of Jesus: "Be compassionate as your Father is compassionate" (Luke 6:36). And again: "The measure you measure out will be measured back to you" (Luke 6:38).

There can be no compassion without passion. There can be no love without suffering. Jesus suffered his passion out of compassion. "No greater love than a person lay down his life for a friend."

Without love, the passion of Jesus makes no sense. Without the passion, Jesus' love for us makes no sense. Passion without compassion is meaningless. Suffering without compassion is unbearable.

To suffer without loving is to despair.

To suffer for the sake of suffering is impossible.

To suffer for the sake of another is sanctity.

To love without suffering is not to love but to like, not friendship but fellowship.

To love without suffering is infatuation.

Giving is another word for suffering. To give until it hurts is no longer giving but loving.

Love is purest when it hurts the most.

Jesus' love was purest when he hung on the cross.

Jesus was happiest when he was dying, a small child once said. In answer to the question "Why, my child?" she responded, "It's because he had to be happiest when he was dying for his friends." God is joy.

"Thank you, Lord, for giving me all the love I need," a small boy once prayed.

He didn't pray for "all the love I want," or for "less than I have," but "for all the love I need."

Thank you, Lord, for giving me all the suffering I need. Not more than I can handle. Not less than I need. If I am to love, I need to suffer. If I suffer, I need to do it out of love.

Jesus died for us. Compassion.

Jesus embraced us on the cross. Forgiveness.

Jesus visited Adam, Eve, and all the other sinners in the netherworld — after his death — to set them free. Mercy.

Compassion, forgiveness, mercy. That is what the cross is all about.

Measure for Measure

JESUS broke out of the tomb to go to Galilee to be with his friends. Friendship.

Jesus overcame death so that we might live. Life.

Jesus died in ignominy but rose to life in glory so that we might be saved. Hope.

Friendship, life, hope. That's what the empty tomb is all about.

There can be no friendship, life, or hope without first compassion, forgiveness, mercy.

There can be no empty tomb without first the cross.

There can be no resurrection without first death.

The measure I measure out will be the measure back to me.

Jesus measured out his life at the moment of his death on the cross. It was measured back to him through his glorious resurrection from the dead.

Jesus measured out compassion in all his actions of ministry. He climaxed that compassion with death on the cross. The Father rewarded him with the complete compassionate act of restoring him to new life. His compassion was measured back to him.

And so will my compassion while on earth be measured back to me at the moment of death. It is then that passion and compassion will embrace and become one in the arms of Jesus.

Rejection

No one suffered rejection more than Jesus. He was rejected by almost everyone as he hung on the cross, except by his Father and a small group of women.

From the very beginning of his life, Jesus was to suffer rejection. Even when he was a Child his parents had to flee into Egypt to save his life.

Jesus, as teacher, was rejected in the synagogues — the usual lot of the prophet. He was rejected even by some of the people he helped — the lepers who did not return to thank him, save one.

Jesus was rejected and betrayed in the end by Judas, denied three times by Peter, forsaken by the Father in the Garden of Gethsemane, rejected even by the disciples at the moment of his crucifixion.

Jesus was rejected by the religious and civil leaders of his time: the Pharisees, the Sadducees, and the Zealots, as well by the officials of the occupying Roman government. From Herod to Pilate, Jesus was rejected and condemned to death.

How did Jesus handle rejection? We turn to the Gospel of Luke.

"Wherever people don't welcome you, leave that town and shake the dust off your feet as a warning to them," he told his twelve disciples when he sent them out to preach the kingdom of God (Luke 9:4). The same happens when he and the disciples prepared to go to a Samaritan town, but were not welcome. "Then Jesus and his disciples went on to another village" (Luke 9:56).

"Anyone who starts to plow and then keeps looking back is of no use to the kingdom of God" (Luke 9:62).

What Jesus is saying: "Don't look back on what could have been, should have been, or in fact was." The past is over. Look at the present situation and move into the future. "Anyone who is not against you is for you" (Luke 9:49-50).

Jesus accepted rejection in various forms as a reality of his life as a prophet. He wasn't overly depressed by it, except at the final moments in Gethsemane, where for a few brief moments he thought the Father himself had let him down. Each of us will experience similar thoughts in our moments of suffering and death. "My God, My God, why hast thou forsaken me?"

The bitter taste of rejection never dampened Jesus' compassionate love for his enemies. Indeed, it is to those who would reject him, so-called enemies along life's way, that Jesus gives his most compassionate words. Even on the cross, "Forgive them, Father, for they know not what they do."

The bittersweet taste seems to remain with us, especially for those to whom we reach out but who seem to reject us in the end. The rejection by his disciples had to be the cruelest blow of all, the deepest kind of suffering for Jesus.

In Luke 6, we hear the stinging words of the compassionate Jesus. In rapid-fire order, the white-hot words flow. Love your enemies, do good to those that hate you, bless those who curse you, pray for those who mistreat you, turn the other cheek, give your shirt off your back. "No, love your enemies and do good to them; lend and expect nothing back. . . . Be merciful just as your Father is merciful" (Luke 6:27-36).

Finally, Jesus tells us not only to love them but to be slow to judge those who reject us. Let God do the judging. "The measure you use for others is the one that God will use for you" (Luke 6:37-38). See the log in your own eye before you look at the speck in your brother's eye.

No examined life will be free from rejection.

Wintertime of Life

A TREE stands outside my window. I am filled with shame as I look at it. I almost avert my eyes. The tree stands naked.

Except for a few remaining leaves, the tree stands like Adam and Eve in the Garden of Eden. It is as though the tree has committed some kind of terrible sin and has been stripped for final judgment.

I don't like to look at naked trees. Naked trees mean wintertime has arrived. Naked trees mean Advent has arrived.

Like a naked tree, I too stand naked before God this

Advent-time of year. Like the naked trees, I too am in the wintertime of life. By now I have been stripped of all my pretenses. I have been exposed. There is nothing God or I don't know about me. Little by little, leaf by leaf, he has stripped me before his eyes. There is nothing I can hide from him, not even my most secret sins.

Advent is standing naked before God in the wintertime of life.

The lush colors of fall are gone. The air is heavy with dampness, and bones are chilled. Everything is bleak outside, somber, still, on hold. Not only the trees but all of nature stands exposed before God this Advent-time of year.

Advent is the arthritis of life. It nags and gnaws at us. It seemingly won't go away. It aches.

There had to be an Advent. There can be no winter without Advent. There can be no Advent without winter. There could be no springtime without Advent. There can be no Easter without Advent. There can be no Easter without Christmas.

There can be no hope without Advent. The naked trees cannot expect a new spring outfit without winter. My naked soul can only linger and languish in a sort of perpetual purgatory if there be no Advent. Without hope, foreboding, listless, empty.

The plaintive cry of the naked tree can be heard in the rustling of the cold winter winds. It is my cry as well. Come, Lord Jesus. Come to me today. Come in your good time. But come. Come now and come again. Keep coming. Give me new life. Cover me over with new foliage.

Give me new shoots, new buds, Remove my nakedness.

Remove my shame and my guilt. Strip away the dead wood, the wilted last leaf of fall. Come, Lord Jesus, shoot of Jesse.

Nature and liturgy come together in a special way this time of year. They conspire together, as though the God of nature uses all of creation to prepare us for the coming of his Son.

For the next several weeks, like the naked tree, we can do nothing but stand exposed in hopeful anticipation for the wondrous miracle of hope when the Son of God becomes man.

Then we can dream of springtime. Wintertime will have

passed. "The night is far spent, the day is at hand." There are a "new heaven and a new earth to come."

Sanctity and Sanity

PEOPLE relate more easily to sinners than to saints. We stand in awe of saints. No one wants to live with a saint.

Jesus loved sinners but hated their sin.

The Church was established to take care of sinners. Saints take care of the Church.

All saints were sinners. Every saint struggled with sin. Sinners think the odor of sanctity stinks. Saints cannot smell it.

Saints are those who knew they were sinners. Sinners are those who thought they were saints.

A saint is one who hates sin. A sinner is one who hates sinners.

Every saint is one who was first and often a sinner. Every sinner was first a saint.

There is a fine line between sanctity and sanity. Most of us fall on either side.

There is no sanity with sanctity. There is no sanctity without sanity.

Sanctity is a state of becoming. Sin is a state of being.

Sinners can become holy. Saints can become sinners.

Advent is a time to seek sanctity, a time to reject sin, a time to be sane. Sin creates insanity. Sanctity produces sanity.

We pray to saints because we know we are sinners. Every saint at one time sinned — and knew it.

Every sinner wants to be a saint — but doesn't know it.

Sinners think they are saints. Saints think they are sinners.

Advent is a time for sinners to become saints, a time for saints to recognize they are sinners.

Advent is a time to prepare for sanctity — by doing the insane.

Advent is a time to get rid of sin — by doing the sane.

Sanctity is goodness in action. Sin is evil in action. Sanity is knowing the difference.

Who is sane and who is insane? Who is holy and who is a sinner?

The insane are convinced they are sane, and that is their insanity.

The holy are convinced they are sinners, and that is their sanctity.

Sinners who acknowledge their sin are sane. Those who don't are not.

There is a thin line between sanctity and sanity.

The one who would be holy must forgo sin. The one who sins forgoes holiness.

A holy one can sin. A sinner can become holy. But a holy sinner is a contradiction in terms.

A sinner become holy is a saint.

How do we become holy? By conquering sin.

How do we conquer sin? By becoming holy.

The mystery of holiness.

Holiness is a mystery. Only the Church can declare a saint. Only God can forgive a sinner.

There are holy people who have not been declared saints. There are sinful people who have not been condemned.

Jesus was condemned but was without sin.

The woman caught in adultery was not condemned but was forgiven.

John and Jesus

JOHN came fasting and preaching repentance. "Turn away from your sins," he said, "because the kingdom of heaven is near."

Jesus came eating and drinking. "The day will come when the bridegroom will be taken away from them. Then they will fast."

The Pharisees, the Sadducees, and the priests were confused.

John said he was not fit to untie the sandals of Jesus. Jesus said there was no greater prophet in all Israel than John.

The kingdom of God is near, said John.

The kingdom of God is now, said Jesus.

Prepare for the kingdom, said John. Be ready.

The bridegroom is already among you, said Jesus. Rejoice and be merry.

There is a time for fasting and a time for feasting, a time for mourning, a time for celebration, a time for burying, a time for marrying.

Advent belongs to John.

Christmas belongs to Jesus.

John was a prophet.

Jesus was a prophet.

John never had any doubts about who he was.

John was not the One who was expected, not he who was to come.

Jesus was the One who was expected: the Messiah, the liberator, the deliverer, Son of Man, Son of God. There was to be no other.

John was certain who he was. He was not all that certain who Jesus was. "Are you the one, or should we expect someone else?" John sent a messenger to ask Jesus.

Jesus replies, "Go back and tell John what you have seen and heard: the blind can see, the lame can walk, those who suffer from dreaded skin diseases are made clean; the dead can hear, the dead are raised to life, and the Good News is preached to the poor."

John now knows Jesus is the one. John's work is finished. Jesus is among his people.

Is it wrong to say there could be no Jesus without John? No love without repentance? No feasting without fasting? No good works without prayer? No death on the cross without suffering?

No priests without prophets? No Peter without Jesus?

No Jesus without John.

No John without Jesus.

No mourning without rejoicing.

No Advent without Christmas.

No love without sacrificing.

No cross without resurrection.

No resurrection without death.

John, the last of the Old Testament prophets, the first of the New.

John and Jesus prophets.

Both must go to Jerusalem to die.

"Jerusalem, Jerusalem. You kill the prophets, you kill the messenger God has sent you."

Jesus cries over Jerusalem.

Jesus fears Jerusalem.

Jesus is put to death in Jerusalem.

Jerusalem condemns him. Jerusalem puts Jesus to death on a cross.

Forgive them, Father, for they know not what they do.

John is put to death in Jerusalem.

John dies over a banquet, he who came fasting.

Jesus dies on a cross, he who came feasting.

John's head is presented on a silver platter.

Jesus' body is nailed to a tree.

Jerusalem, Jerusalem. "How many times I wanted to put my arms around all your people, just as a hen gathers her chickens under her wings."

Take and Receive

As Christmas draws near, asking and receiving seem to be the major themes, especially for children, as they are filled with expectancy over what they are about to receive for Christmas. But not even adults are immune from asking and seeking this time of year.

"Ask, and you will receive; seek, and you will find; knock, and the door will be opened to you" (Luke 11:9).

First of all, there is a difference between asking and seeking. It seems less demeaning to me as a human person to seek than to ask. Asking can be humbling. It is akin to begging, whereas seeking puts a burden upon me to get involved in the process, not just passively to ask. It is easier to ask than to seek.

Jesus knows what I need. Do I need to ask or beg, if he is my friend, or can I count on him to provide without my asking?

A lover anticipates the needs of the beloved, so that the beloved need not ask and perhaps be embarrassed or demeaned. The lover takes the burden from the beloved by anticipating and providing without the need for asking. Isn't Jesus attentive? Doesn't he anticipate my needs? I have always felt that Jesus knows my needs before I do.

The lover showers the beloved with small gifts, to show he or she is thinking of the beloved. Gifts come as surprises, off guard, spontaneously. Doesn't Jesus do the same? If he loves me, as I know he does, I am sure of this. If he wants to surprise me on this retreat with a gift, I'll accept it but not ask for it or seek it. I'll be grateful and enjoy.

What do I want from Jesus this vacation? I'll leave it up to him. Maybe I have already received enough. Maybe Jesus wants to take something away from me to bring me closer to his heart. Maybe the fact that I am here is enough. I recall going on a vacation with a friend this summer. It was a joy in itself — a special gift to me. A retreat is my vacation with Jesus. It may be his gift to me. I have already received my gift in my closeness to Jesus this week.

So back to prayer. I find it easier to ask and seek something for others than for myself. I need to bombard the heavens for my loved ones. I want them to have a friend in Jesus, as I do. I can pray for that. At a minimum, I want them to see Jesus in me, in my relations with them. Luke (11:28) quotes Jesus as saying, "Blessed , . . are they who hear the word of God and keep it." I could pray for no more than this.

"Take and receive." I like that. I like "take" as a word more than "ask." Take what God has given me — his constant gifts and providence, everything I am and hope to be: talents, experiences, priesthood, the gifts of baptism, and the sacraments that flow from it. Take and receive his gifts rather than ask and beg him to satisfy my needs. His gifts — his graces and blessings — are enough for me.

In return I give back to him all that I am. *Totus Tuus*, as Pope

John Paul II is fond of saying. All yours. Take and receive.

Waiting, Waiting, Waiting

ADVENT is a time to prepare ourselves for the coming of the Lord, but it is also a time of waiting.

Waiting, waiting, waiting. Did you ever stop to think about how much of your life is spent waiting?

I am thinking of poor people in our urban centers waiting in long lines at welfare offices, unemployment offices, and soup lines. I am thinking of mothers and fathers in courtrooms waiting for the trial of a son to be called, followed by the endless continuances, endless hours of coming back to court.

I am thinking of young people waiting weeks and months in jail for their cases to be called — because their families cannot afford bail to get them out. I am thinking of all the hostages who finally have been released from Lebanon, after six to eight years in confinement.

I am thinking of the terminally ill in hospitals, of AIDS patients, awaiting death; of frightened people awaiting major operations; of families waiting in hospital lounges outside of operating room, in intensive care units, or in emergency wards.

I am thinking of the elderly in nursing homes waiting for relatives or friends to visit them, of parents waiting up all night for their teenage children to come home from a dance.

I am thinking of pregnant women waiting for their babies to be born, or the anxiety of fathers and grandparents.

Waiting, anticipation, fear, hope, despondency, disappointment, hurt — all mingled together in our lives in one way or another as we wait, hoping for the best, fearful of the worst.

We live in a frenetic, frantic world, always on the go, too busy, too active, on the run either at work or jogging after work. We are impatient. Things never move fast enough. We never get caught up. We never get it all done, whether at home or at work or at play.

Then it happens. Unexpectedly, we have to wait. Something inevitably happens in our lives to slow us down, put us on hold.

Each of us must take inventory of our lives to verify this. The details change, the end is the same. Somewhere we will just have to wait — for a job, a raise, a promotion, a doctor's report, a judge's verdict, a baby, a friend's visit, a relative, a break, an answer to a prayer, to catch a fish or enjoy a sunset, to prepare a meal or fulfill a dream, for the leaves to fall, the snow to melt, the buds to open, the fog to lift, the sun to shine.

Life is a series of expectations, hopes, dreams, disappointments, delays — from traffic jams to golden years.

Waiting. Waiting. Waiting.

That's what this season of Advent is all about. We are waiting for the Lord to come. We are impatient, anxious, fearful, hopeful. Hopeful that we will be ready when he comes, that we will be calm, expectant, ready, unafraid.

Advent teaches us — the Church teaches us — to be patient, to learn how to wait, how to stand in line.

If Advent teaches us anything, it is how to wait, how to anticipate, how to expect, how to hope, how to slow down, how to reflect, how to cope.

Put another way, Advent teaches us how to pray. Prayer is stepping back, changing pace, reevaluating, putting things in perspective, accepting God's ways as not being our ways.

Prayer is making a commitment, saying *"Fiat"* with the Virgin Mother of Jesus. "Thy will be done," let it happen, let it be.

Patience and Prayer

IN the Advent Scriptures, it is St. Paul who picks up on the theme of patience. Isaiah already has drawn up a powerful picture of the peace and tranquillity which will be inaugurated when the Savior, descendant of David, root of Jesse, comes among us.

It is Isaiah who whets our appetite for the coming of Jesus when he describes life on God's holy mountain, where there will be nothing harmful or evil. There "wolves and sheep will live together in peace, and leopards will lie down with young goats, calves and lion cubs will feed together, and little children will take care of them."

O Lord, how long must we wait? We grow impatient. "O Come, O Come, Emmanuel" is our Advent song.

St. Paul cautions patience. The coming of Jesus will inaugurate the kingdom of God, but it will not be until the Second Coming of Jesus, his return at the end of time, that the vision of Isaiah will be fully accomplished. It is that period of human history between the first and the second coming of Jesus that we who are the People of God, his chosen ones, will make it happen. No magic wand will bring about the harmony among all of creation that Isaiah and Paul sing about. In reality, if there is to be any measure of international and domestic peace on earth and in our time, the People of God, imbued with the teachings of Christ, will have to bring it about.

Isaiah has the vision. Paul tells us how to turn it into reality. And finally, in the Gospel of St. Matthew today, we are introduced to John the Baptist, who is the bridge between Isaiah and Jesus. It is John who calls us to reform our lives so that we can bear fruit.

The Feast of the Immaculate Conception of Mary is not strictly an Advent feast, but fortunately, this long-standing feast of the Virgin Mary comes on December 8, the beginning of the Advent season.

Isaiah, the proto-evangelist, centuries before any of the four evangelists would write, picked up on the Good News: "A virgin shall conceive and bear a son and his name shall be called Emmanuel — God with us."

December 8 is Mary's day. She fills our hearts and our minds. She overwhelms us with her gentle faith. Because of her, the Advent story can now unfold until that other moment outside the little town of Bethlehem when Mary will have her Baby. Let us rejoice. Blessed are you among women.

But never let us forget that Mary is exalted for the sake of Jesus. John Henry Newman wrote over a hundred years ago that "it was fitting that Mary, as being a creature, though first of creatures, should have an office of ministration. She, as others, came into the world to do a work, she had a mission to fulfill; her grace and her glory are not for her own sake, but for the maker's; and to her is committed the custody of the Incarnation . . . her glories and devotions paid to her proclaim and define the right faith concerning him as God and man."

Listening, Listening

IF Advent is a time of waiting, then waiting is a time of listening. Waiting is downtime. There is not much we can do actively when we are waiting for someone or for something to happen. The preparations have been made, and now we must wait for the events to unfold.

During Advent we have been asked simply to wait and then wait some more, and the Lord will come. We must be quiet, on the alert, full of anticipation, but, nonetheless, "wait." It tries our patience.

Today's liturgy suggests that while waiting, also, ever so quietly, we should listen. Let the voices speak to us. Voices in the wilderness, voices from the desert, voices from the present. We must clear our lives of the clutter and the noises around us in order to listen.

Voices in the wilderness. We sometimes hear them, but we really don't want to. They are faraway echoes of our deepest selves, and so we are frightened by them. They irritate us, disturb our ease, rub us wrong, persist, sometimes ever so softly, other times with a violence that shatters our composure. They come upon us like the wind.

Isaiah reassures us today. The desert will give way to abundant flowers. The feeble will be made strong. The eyes of the blind will be opened. The deaf will hear, and the lame will walk. The Lord will come in glory. Sorrow and mourning will flee. And Jesus reassures John the Baptist that "the blind have recovered their sight, cripples walk, lepers are cured, the deaf hear, the dead are raised to life, and the poor have the Good News preached to them."

The voice of Isaiah has been heard.

Voices from the wilderness. I hear the voices of my children crying out for help; the voices of the sick and the dying; of those in troubled marriages, the divorced, the widow and the widower; the wounded healers who are our ministers. Are you listening to me?

But loudest of all this season, I hear the voice of John the Baptist, no, not the Messiah, not Elijah, not Moses, but the voice of the wilderness prophet. There he stands, perhaps unknown to us, no more than a slave whose task it is to untie the master's sandal, unworthy even for that, a voice in the desert, crying out, "Make straight the way of the Lord."

When I hear his voice, peace and joy settle over me. It is then that I understand all those other voices in the wilderness. The Lord wants me, they sing in concert, to bring glad tidings to the lowly, Good News to the poor, to heal the brokenhearted.

The Lord is calling me to join him in making justice and peace spring up before all nations, for kindness and truth to embrace, an unlikely odd couple, kindness tenderly bending down to embrace an unbending truth.

John preached a hard line. "Repent," cut down on your food and drink, get rid of excess material baggage, fast, simplify your lifestyle, tighten your belts, be ready and waiting — an unbending truth.

But the softer message comes from Jesus. Truth will be tempered by compassion. Jesus is the anointed one who preached the Good News to the poor. It is Jesus who is the bending, kind one, who promises mercy. It is Jesus who bends down tenderly to embrace the unbending John. The voices in the wilderness have been heard by the tenderhearted Jesus. The work of salvation is already begun.

Today we rejoice. We exalt with joy in the Good News brought to us.

Joseph and Jesus

THIS day, as we begin our final days of preparations for the birth of Jesus, belongs to Joseph. Our Advent liturgy rightfully focuses on Isaiah, John the Baptist, and Mary, as they dominate our preparations for the birth of Jesus. So much so that we tend to forget, overlook, or put into the background the role of Joseph, who is also caught up in the drama of our salvation. We almost lose sight of Joseph, as he blends into the landscape.

"Why me, Lord? Why Mary?" These and a hundred similar questions must have raced through this good and honest and religious Jewish man's mind. The incredible part of it was not that God could decide to bring about the birth of his only Son, but that he would choose such simple, uncomplicated, unknown, anonymous, ordinary people as the instrument of our salvation. But why, Lord, did you reach down into the small village of Nazareth to choose a workman and his young bride to reconcile heaven and earth?

The Child is born. Joseph becomes the obedient father. He takes care of Mary, and he takes care of the Boy Jesus.

Certainly, not an easy life for Joseph. But because of his deep faith in God, Joseph can endure the ordeal in Bethlehem, the flight into Egypt, the return to Nazareth where he will raise his family and tend to the young Jesus until he is thirty, teach him a trade, instruct him in the Scriptures, and raises a very unusual, blessed, and gifted Child.

Joseph does his best. He is a good foster father, a loving father to his adopted son. What shines through his life are faith, justice, sensitivity to God's voice, obedience, fidelity to his wife, hard work and self-support. In relations with Jesus, he is a supportive father and encouraging.

No, it was not an easy life, but it was a peaceful life even to death, and a steady life. Joseph is the good husband, very protective of Mary, faithful and loyal, provident, God-fearing and solicitous. Joseph is a good Jewish father and a good Jewish husband.

Joseph's relationship to Jesus is all the more difficult given the fact that Jesus' real Father is in heaven, to whom Jesus will pray, love and pay heed, not his earthly foster father, Joseph. "He who comes from above is greater than all. He who comes from the earth belongs to the earth and speaks about earthly things," John tells us. "The Father loves his Son and his put everything in his power. Whoever believes in the Son has eternal life; whoever disobeys the Son will not have life, but will remain under God's punishment."

He who knows the Father knows the Son, and he who knows the Son knows the Father. Jesus can say this about his heavenly Father, but not about Joseph. There are some things Joseph can never share. Jesus is born of a virgin mother and a divine Father, and so he is unique in human history, both God and man, Son of God and Son of Mary, human and divine. Jesus can never share this special relationship with Joseph.

So our dear foster father, Joseph, remains an outsider, yet a privileged insider. He, of all men, has been given custody of Jesus during his formative years. His vocation, too, is unique and it is surrounded with mystery.

It was Joseph's great faith, along with Mary's *Fiat*, that brought all this about.

Ordinary Day, Extraordinary Night

THE day Jesus was born was an ordinary day for Joseph and Mary, but what an extraordinary night it brought for the world! The ordinary and the extraordinary, how often they join together in our own lives!

In order to speak about the events of Christmas Day, we are required to use everyday words, the less pompous the better. A little Baby born to us, so humble, so poor, so like the others. Yet we need the sublime words, the extraordinary words, that reveal the infinite depths of God, since God himself is present in this trembling flesh. This tiny creature is the One who was prophesied, the expected One, the One who has finally come. God himself has appeared and dwells among us.

Let us reread the account of Jesus' birth to see what an ordinary day it was.

There was a worldwide census taking place, ordered by Caesar Augustus. Everyone went to register, each to his own town. Joseph and Mary were no different from anyone else. They went from Nazareth in Galilee to Bethlehem in Judea, David's town, because Joseph was of the family of David.

The Scriptures are very sparse in detail, telling us that while Joseph and Mary were in Bethlehem, Mary had her Baby. Since they could find no lodging, she had her Baby where animals were kept. We can reconstruct the day.

They probably arrived in Bethlehem in the morning by donkey. Joseph checked out a few places to stay. Nothing available. Mary probably got a little tense over it all, what with the Baby due any moment. They probably did their civic duty — registering — then stopped for a little lunch, which Mary more than likely packed for the trip. Finally, they moved outside the town to try to find a place to stay. As it turned out, the only place available was a stable.

An ordinary day, with its ups and downs, disappointments, probably some fussing. Hundreds of people in Bethlehem at that time spent a very similar day.

Then it happened. Mary had her Baby. The ordinary day was climaxed by an extraordinary event that would turn human history upside down and give dawn to a new era.

The Scriptures continue but now the mood changes.

There are shepherds tending their flocks. An angel appears to them and the glory of God is around them. The angel puts their fears to rest. "Fear nothing. This is good news. A Savior has been born. You will find him in swaddling clothes."

Then the heavens break out in song. Can we grasp the magnitude of this simple birth in a manger on a hillside of Bethlehem before simple shepherds and animals under the stars? Can we grasp the poverty of the situation, the poverty of circumstances surrounding the event, against the power of the moment? Poverty and power side by side?

How good it is that all these events took place outside the city of Bethlehem, under the stars and moon, in the presence of the shepherds and their flocks, to the singing of the angels. How uneventful it would have been had Mary had her Baby in a small, stuffy room in the inn, in private.

All creation groaned for this day when the Promised One would come. Eight centuries before, the prophet Isaiah proclaimed this coming of God among us.

Now it happens.

My dear friends, this night place yourself in the scene at Bethlehem. You are a bystander who came to Bethlehem to take part in the census. You are a Jew who is steeped in the sacred writings contained in the Torah. You know the book of Isaiah inside and out, from memory. You know the current political situation of your country, which is now occupied and under Roman rule. The future, indeed, looks bleak.

Then you come to the scene outside of Bethlehem. The angels singing, the quiet and peace, the simple shepherds, the warmth of the animals. All of creation comes alive.

You sense the mystery of the night, the poignancy of the moment.

You see the strength and the care of the foster father, Joseph; the tenderness of the virgin mother, Mary; the glow on the face of the Baby, Jesus.

This, indeed, is an extraordinary night at the end of a very ordinary day. It is creation day all over again. God has relented and forgiven his people and fulfilled his promise. A savior is born among us.

At this moment, let us recall Isaiah, when earlier in Advent he predicted the lion would lie down with the kid. Recall John the Baptist, who called us to reform our lives, to be prepared, for we know not the day nor the hour. Recall Jesus' message to John: The lame will walk, the deaf hear, the blind see, and the poor will have the Good News preached to them.

Recall Joseph's trust and Mary's "I will."

Now, this night, it all comes together outside the little town of Bethlehem.

God is, indeed, with his people.

What Kind of Child?

THE celebration of Christmas is winding down. Crumpled wrapping paper and tattered tinsel have been gathered from beneath the Christmas trees. Relatives are returning to their homes. Children already are growing weary of their new toys. And the leftover turkey has all but disappeared from the refrigerator.

The night of nights for the Holy Family has given away to the dawn of a new age in history. True, the Holy Family is still lingering in Bethlehem until Mary and Child are able to travel. Soon they will be visited by the three kings from afar. But what is next for the Holy Family after the circumcision of Jesus and the presentation of the Child in the Temple of Jerusalem?

Will Joseph return to Nazareth and take up the simple life as a carpenter, husband, and now father? What dramatic effect, if any, will the birth of Jesus have on the lifestyle of the Holy Family? We already know the answers to some of these questions, but at this moment Joseph and Mary do not. They await the guidance of God.

Our young families today, I am sure, have some of the feelings that Joseph and his young wife experienced on the birth of their firstborn Child. What will this child be? And for a first child, the anxiety is even greater. What kind of child, O Lord, have you given us? Now a radical new lifestyle begins for them. All attention, twenty-four hours a day, becomes focused on the needs of this tiny, helpless infant, and young couples become ever so solicitous.

Christmas has come and gone, the preparations so long, the celebrations so short. For those of us who have just begun to take down the Christmas decorations, the time after Christmas can often be a very lonely time.

The heart feels this emptiness. In the twinkle of a Christmas light, many of us again stand face to face with the stark realities of life. Our hearts almost instinctively leap to spring and Easter, when the Lord will arise from his long, dark night of the soul on Easter Sunday, and, we hope, family and friends will gather again.

John Henry Newman has reminded us that the great events in the Life of Jesus took place in obscurity, in secret, all except his death. "The Annunciation was secret; the Nativity was secret; the fasting in the wilderness was secret; and the Resurrection and Ascension of Jesus into heaven were not far from secret. One thing alone was public, his death on the cross, which in the eyes of the world, was not a sign of power, but of weakness."

Most secret of all was the flight of the Holy Family into Egypt. Yes, the Holy Family, when Jesus was still a newborn Baby, had to steal away into the night to escape into Egypt, or risk the Child's being killed by King Herod.

The flight into Egypt had to be a very frightening, traumatic and unexpected journey for Joseph, Mary and the Baby Jesus. They were a refugee family. Because of political conditions and the fear of death, they had to flee their own country, leave behind their own home and belongings, and put down roots as aliens in a foreign country.

We have scant details on this perilous trip into Egypt, but it takes little imagination to realize it had to be a very difficult time.

Eventually, of course, the Holy Family will return to Nazareth, after the death of Herod.

Not every day can be Christmas.

On the Way of the Cross:
The Stations

I. Jesus is condemned to death

To be condemned to anything is hell. To be condemned to death is the pits. To be condemned to live in a ghetto, a rat-infested tenement or refugee camp, in a wind-whipped tent in a drought- stricken part of Africa, in a latrine-busted prison cell, or even in a bad marriage is humiliating and depersonalizing. To be condemned implies a certain finality. A no-win, hopeless situation. To be condemned to death, whether by a court, a doctor, a political system, is the ultimate desecration.

Dear Jesus, you who experienced condemnation, conviction, be merciful to those who have been condemned, not always justly, to a dehumanized life in a world that convicts for crimes uncommitted. Work your justice for them. To be unjustly condemned is the worst affliction of all.

II. Jesus picks up his cross

IT doesn't look too big at first glance, but is heavier than it looks. After all, I'm still feeling pretty good. I can carry it, I think. At least I can pick it up.

Funny looking thing, isn't it? Why those crossbars? It doesn't fit me very well. I just don't know where to grab hold of it. Which end? Should I drag it?

Burdens are never tailor-made. They are never comfortable, or they wouldn't be unbearable. We are never quite ready for them. Life was pretty nice as it was. Why the interruption? Why did it happen now?

Dear Jesus, why war, why hunger and starvation? Why violence, why floods or drought or earthquakes, why disaster, why sudden death? It seemed we were going to make it, now we are uprooted again. So much uncertainty. Help me, Lord Jesus, to pick up this cross, get it by the right end. If I can pick it up, I may be able to carry it.

III. Jesus falls for the first time

THE first time wasn't bad. I am still feeling strong. I am fresh into the ordeal. I don't know what is down the road. I can pick myself up and start anew. Who knows, the chemotherapy treatment may work. Maybe the AIDS virus won't kick in. Who knows, I may gather strength. Hope springs eternal. Ask any person facing a terminal disease. The first fall isn't too difficult. The burden isn't all that heavy yet — I am confident I can handle it.

Dear Jesus, countless thousands of your people have made the first step, survived the first fall, but found it the beginning of fear, anxiety, suffering. Some may never make it alive. Dear Jesus, help me make it home. The family needs me.

IV. Jesus meets his mother

GOD, I wasn't prepared for this. The cross is heavy enough without exposing it my mother. She had her share of crosses with me. She doesn't need to see me with this one. I was hoping to sneak away without telling her. Look, I want to come home someday, but not looking like this — bedraggled, confused, unkempt, angry with the world, broken, and beaten. That's no way for my family to see me, especially my mother. Oh, I know she wants to share it all. That's what mothers are all about.

Dear Jesus, running away from home is hard enough, being forced to start anew in another strange city is not my wish, but to expose this to my family is too much. Help me make it painless for them. Help them to understand that I'll come home someday and show them a better life. Make it easy for mama.

V. Simon helps Jesus

THANK God for Simon. I needed him. Thank God for mission stations in the wilderness, thank God for emergency relief programs worldwide — Catholic Relief Services, Refugee Services, Red Cross, Care, countless others — or self-help programs at home: the Campaign for Human Development, CETA, Catholic Charities, and what's left of government social programs.

Dear Jesus, I thought I could make it alone. Once I got up from the first fall, I thought I had my second wind. But you don't know — or do you? — what a lift Simon has given my spirits. I might just make it after all — with your help. But God, it's rough out there.

VI. Veronica wipes the face of Jesus

I DIDN'T think I'd ever need the help of a nurse. I guess I never expected to find one out there, even if I needed one. I hoped to have my own baby in a refugee camp, but I had visions of never reaching one in time. I thought I would have my baby at the last little village near the border, until the soldiers appeared. So I kept moving.

Where did this wonderful nun-nurse come from? How did she get to this little God-forsaken camp along the Salvadoran border? What kind of fire burns within her?

Dear Jesus, the gentle touch of your wonderful servant was almost too much to expect. First there was Simon, now Veronica. My hopes are buoyed (no puns, please) with my newborn boy to accompany me. Where do I go from here, still condemned to death?

VII. Jesus falls the second time

WHAT a letdown after Simon and Veronica! I thought I could lick the world. This disappointment hurts. Isn't America the land of the free? I mistakenly thought that once I reached the borders of Thailand I was in America. Now I know better. It takes time — maybe forever. I don't have refugee status. I am still an alien. I can't go anywhere until someone sponsors me. And I know no one in America. I may never leave this camp — this ghetto.

Dear Jesus, waiting will be difficult, all so unproductive; so dependent on others, no chance to grow and develop and move on my own. I hate the welfare system, the unemployment, the handouts. Help me break these shackles, Lord.

VIII. Jesus speaks to the daughters of Jerusalem

WE had a good cry together. I am not alone in my suffering. These women, like Simon and Veronica, have helped me work through my anger, my frustration, my resentment. I needed the therapy of a good cry, a good self-look. I am not the only one out there carrying a cross. Damn the alcohol, the drugs, the self-inflicted wounds. That's not the way to escape or to heal the wounds inflicted by others. I've got to get hold of myself and be a person about all this.

Dear Jesus, that was a downer! I never should have gotten mixed up with all those dudes, but thank you for the therapy session. I am back on the road again. The cross is still heavy, but I am not feeling guilty anymore. I am in touch with reality again.

IX. Jesus falls the third time

HOW I wanted to stay down this time, just throw in the towel. I'd prayed I'd die, never get up again. Why try again? Three strikes and you are out. That was my third fall, and each time it is more difficult to get up. This time I had to get up alone — no Simon, no Veronica, no women along the wayside to help — just me.

I think you are telling me something. I was getting too dependent on help from the outside. If I am going to be a person — and get over this prolonged adolescent stage of dependency — I'd better draw on some inner strength.

Dear Jesus, thanks for the healing, for the grace to leave the house, look for a job, start to get my act together one more time. The recession isn't going to end in any foreseeable future.

X. Jesus is stripped of his garments

IT is the ultimate humiliation. I'm so vulnerable, especially when I am naked before these animals. I know what is going to happen next. I can feel them rushing at me — snarling, laughing, moaning, with their sodden bodies and foul breath. God, it is going to be terrible, I am too frail to resist, and too exhausted. It will all go on the records at the police interrogation. I'll be called a Communist pig for caring for the poor. I'll be beaten and shipped back to the mother house with orders never to come back to this small mission outpost again.

Dear Jesus, the final straw. What more can I offer up to you than my virginity, unless it be life itself. Accept my naked, ravaged body, what's left of it, and let it be an offering for my poor friends and neighbors for a better tomorrow.

XI. Jesus is nailed to the cross

I'M really not conscious anymore, just drifting in and out, with a terrible sadness overwhelming me, impressions from the past swirling around. Why the violence? So much terrorism and violence in the world today: terrorism in Lebanon and Iraq; recently in the Persian Gulf, Northern Ireland, Yugoslavia; death squads in El Salvador; abortions; violence in Chicago streets — on and on: sadistic acts of violence, with no respect for life. I am all these victims at this moment.

Dear Jesus, all the violence of the centuries is being pounded into these hands and feet, all the spilled blood of the innocent is gushing through those nail holes, now and forever more. Is it any less barbarous today, after two thousand years of Christianity, than it was on Golgotha? Any more civilized?

XII. Jesus dies on the cross

WAS it a great put-on — getting me up three times with that cross, meeting Simon, Veronica, and the women, getting my hopes up? And now this. Here I am on that stupid cross I carried to the bitter end, only to be nailed to it, and now to die on it?

I should have seen it coming. I had been condemned to it. But

I thought I could beat it, find a way out, escape the system, strike a blow for innocence. Justice will surely win in the end. Yeah, justice.

Dear Jesus, it's over. My fight is finished. I am the all-time big loser. You might as well pull the plug, call in the family, make the burial plans. I don't want it to end this way, but so be it. Catch you later.

XIII. Jesus is taken down from the cross

I ALWAYS wanted to attend my own funeral to see who my friends were. I never would have guessed it of Joseph of Arimathea and Nicodemus — not exactly my closest friends and not even family. Somehow I must have made an impact on them.

So it is all over now, except for the ones left behind. Now they must get over their grief, pick up the pieces of what was our life, and start anew. I hope they are not mad at me for leaving them. God knows I fought as hard as I could to stay alive, but the cancer just ran it course; no stopping it. The chemotherapy was no picnic for me, either. Sooner or later we all have to die. It was sooner for me.

Dear Jesus, be kind and gentle with my survivors. Send Simon and Veronica and the sorrowing women of Jerusalem into their lives as they try to heal some of the wounds left in my absence.

XIV. Jesus is placed in a sepulcher

IF I could come back for just a few moments, I'd tell them about life in a sepulcher. I didn't waste any time there — or I should I say eternity? I was long gone.

I got the big picture now. When I was condemned to death, I was promised life. When I picked up that cross, I was headed home. When I fell under the weight of that cross, I was being me. When I got up, I was reaching for the stars. When I met those good people along the way who helped me, I was meeting Jesus. When I was humiliated and nailed to that cross, I was part of the drama, the salvation of the world. When I died I found new life, free from injustice, poverty, alienation, dehumanization, violence — and death.

The Death of Jesus

PLACE yourself in this scene. We are at a wake service. Jesus has died on the cross. His body has been prepared for burial. He has been laid in the tomb.

We are gathered together in this austere upper chamber as friends and family of Jesus. We are here with Peter, James, John, and the rest of the disciples, the holy women, Mary the Mother of Jesus, Mary Magdalene, Martha, Lazarus, Nicodemus, Joseph of Arimathea. We are here with all of them.

It is a time of sadness, mourning, tears, emptiness, hollow feelings in the pits of our stomachs, a dryness of throat, of overwhelming grief. We are in disarray, because of a loss of direction, a lack of leadership, and an absence of companionship.

Death hangs heavy in the air, as if some great tragedy has struck in our lives. We go about embracing one another, holding one another's hand, caring for one another, exchanging condolences, retelling memories.

It is a time of extraordinary grief. We are in the dampness of this austere upper room. No flowers, no joy, no celebration. It is an almost interminable time of waiting for what we know not, for something to happen to break the gloom, lift our depression, reenergize our spirits.

And so we bargain for time. We have lost our appetites, we are thirsty, we are spiritually and emotionally drained.

We had experienced the intimacy of the Last Supper with Jesus last evening in this very room. Did he not share everything with us, even his body and blood? Did he not bathe our feet in a final gesture of love?

Now he is dead. It all went so quickly. It was so cruel, so unfair, so bitter, so nasty. And we stood helplessly by to allow history to do its thing.

In this cold upper chamber, today we have remembered "what we have seen with our very eyes, what we heard, and what our hands touched."

We listened to Isaiah try to explain the events to us. "It was our infirmities that he bore, our sufferings that he endured. While we thought of him as stricken, as one smitten by God and afflicted, but he was pierced for our offenses, crushed for our sins."

We sang the Passion account of John in oh-so-soulful, mournful, subdued tones, as we relived in every detail Jesus' trial, suffering, and death.

Now we will conclude our wake service with prayers of supplication, with a visit to the wood of the cross of Jesus, after an ever-so-light repast, empty of celebration, as we take within us the Body and Blood of Jesus.

The wake is over. We go outside into the night to be by ourselves, to cry quietly in the darkness, to be alone with our grief and our sadness, to penetrate the meaning of these life-giving events. We shall not be afraid to cry, to let it all hang out.

Today is a day for grieving. Tomorrow will bring new hope.

The Resurrection of Jesus

I HAD to get out somehow. There was no way I could be contained by that barren tomb. I had to find a way out, simply because that's what my Father had promised me. If death were the end, then all mankind before me and down through the centuries since then, through time to eternity, would have been victims of a gigantic fraud perpetrated by God the day he created the world.

If suffering and death — and mine wasn't that bad compared to the suffering of many of the others — were the final note, where is hope, where is justice? In fact, where is faith? At least I didn't linger. Three hours on the cross wasn't three years of slow death through cancer or AIDS, or three months in Auschwitz.

But I had to be victorious over death. We all do, if only to bring hope to all the little people in the world who suffer poverty, disease, indignity, violence. How would the scales of justice ever balance, if the tomb were the end?

I am amused by all those stories explaining the empty tomb — how my friends sneaked me out, or how they hallucinated all my later appearances to them after my death. I guess the news media had to find some reason to disbelieve the single truth that I rose from the dead. I understand their cynicism. For someone to overcome death, to rise again with new life, is pretty heady stuff. It should have been the biggest news event of all history. But the press is a doubting Thomas by nature, and that is okay with me.

The thing is, I told them ahead of time what was going to happen. I leaked the story. Like it was no big surprise, but even friends and family didn't believe me. That walk to Emmaus was amusing, in a way. Here I am walking with two of my closest friends, and explaining the scriptures to them, and they didn't have a clue as to who I was.

No one seems to believe in miracles. God knows I performed enough of them while I was alive, but my friends never got the message. Why was the miracle of my resurrection so unbelievable, after what I did for Lazarus?

There was a pattern to my life, from the day of my conception. Everything I did prepared me for breaking out of that tomb. There was just no way my life was going to end there. My Father knew it, and he told me the same. The Old Testament prophets knew it. They predicted it. Everyone who came before me knew it.

The people of the Third World suffering poverty and violence and repression believe it. Poor people living in ghettos, whether Jews or Arabs, blacks or Chicanos, believe it. Haitians, Cuban refugees, Indochinese refugees, Central American refugees, East African refugees, East European refugees, believe it.

I don't care what part of the world, or what race, or what religion or state in life, from the first days of creation until tomorrow, good people everywhere believe I had to break out of that tomb.

The tomb was confining. I couldn't breathe freely inside it. I couldn't see or hear or smell or feel or touch a thing. I couldn't grow. I was hemmed in, just lying there dead. Was I just going to rot away, become part of the earth, and that would be the end? No way.

Call it what you will, Easter, or Sunday, or "that great getting-up morning" or Resurrection Day, whatever. It all comes down to one word: hope — hope in a better tomorrow, hope for a better world, hope in a life hereafter, a day of reconciliation, or justice, or fullness of life. Call it whatever, it means freedom, liberation, fulfillment, and one day it will come into the life of each of us.

The day you die is the day you begin to live, freed from all the limitations and encumbrances of this world, free from the constrictions of time and place, freed from the alibis that you never became what you wanted to be.

Why do I say this? Because I pushed back that crazy stone some 2,000 years ago and walked out of that tomb alive. I had been dead, but now I live. Because I live, so will you. Believe me.

Second Spring

THE long dark night of the soul is over.

The darkness that enshrouded the world at the moment of the death of Jesus has been pierced by a bright new life.

Nature is seething within with stirrings of new life.

Flashes of hope, like bolts of lightning, pierce the clouds.

New waters, like dew drops unpolluted, wash the earth clean.

The smell of eucalyptus fills the air.

The mustard seed, God's tiniest, pokes its tiny shoot through the rain-softened earth, destined to become the largest of trees.

The clouds part and a multi-colored rainbow bridges the sky to unite east and west.

Spring has arrived. It is Easter Sunday. Our Lord and Savior, as he promised, has risen from the dead, and we along with all creation have come alive again. That which was dead is alive. We who were dead have resurrected.

The stone of that cold, dark, damp, musty tomb has been rolled back.

And suddenly, our churches, which yesterday had been only somber, barren tombs, have come alive with the growth of spring, fresh flowers, warm lights, festive sounds, and alleluias unending. There is rejoicing in the air, as birds are singing and the sun is shining.

Our Lord and Savior has risen from the tomb. He has lifted the veil of darkness. He has set us free to soar with the Spirit.

"Do our hearts not pound," as he fills us with new hope, new zeal for the kingdom? Death is no longer our conqueror but a passport to life eternal. We too shall live again.

Now it is the new Jesus, the glorified Jesus, the triumphant Jesus, who takes us by the hand to lead us to the new Jerusalem, where the banquet is prepared and where we shall drink only the best of wines.

Nearly one hundred fifty years ago in England, the great Anglican convert Venerable John Henry Newman preached on "The Second Spring." He pointed to the material world around us as an example of the cycle of death and life. "The sun sinks to rise again: the day is swallowed up in the gloom of night, to be born out of it, as fresh as if it had never been quenched. Spring passes into Summer and Autumn into Winter, only by its own return to triumph over the grave, towards which it hastened from its first hour."

"Man rises to fall. He was young, he is old, he is now young again. He is born to die.

"The noblest efforts of our genius, the conquests we have made, the nations we have civilized outlive us, but in the end tend to dissolution.

"Mankind and all his works are mortal. They die."

Not so the Church, Newman says, born from the very side of Christ this week. For the Church, the past returns; the dead live. It is the coming of the Second Spring. For the Church, there is death but always new life, as it is for the Christian. Yesterday we were dead. Today we are alive. Because of the death and resurrection of Jesus, the Church constantly renews us and through us renews itself.

"The world grows old, but the Church is ever young."

The Miracle of Easter

EASTER Sunday is the feast day of liberation.

There are those who would separate liberation from redemption.

A theology that focuses on the cross, on the suffering and death of Jesus, is as incomplete as a theology that focuses solely on the resurrection of Jesus. We can no more separate the cross from the empty tomb than we can separate the crucifixion from the resurrection of Jesus.

Without the cross there could have been no empty tomb. Without death there can be no resurrection. Without the reality of sin, there would have been no need for redemption. Without Good Friday, there can be no Easter Sunday.

Without oppression there can be no liberation. Easter is the day of liberation. Liberation from what? From death. From sin. From doubt. From injustice.

Easter Sunday is a day of reaffirmation, reintegration, reunion.

Reaffirmation means hope. Reintegration means wholeness. Reunion means God and person together again in full relationship.

The miracle of Easter ought not to shock us. The shattering reality is that had Jesus not risen, had the tomb been the end, then nothing would have made sense.

The message Jesus preached demanded an Easter. The kingdom Jesus preached demanded an Easter.

First, the message, which was given at a synagogue of Nazareth, when Jesus concretized all the hopes of his people. " 'The spirit of the Lord is upon me, therefore he has anointed me. He has sent me to bring glad tidings to the poor, to proclaim liberty to captives, recovery of sight to the blind, and release to prisoners, to announce a year of favor from the Lord.'. . . Today's scripture passage is fulfilled in your hearing" (Luke 4:18-21).

Jesus presents himself as a liberator. Without Easter, Jesus would have had to become a revolutionary, or a politician, or a pacifist to fulfill the Scripture passage. He came instead as a servant, not a messianic king.

Some today still claim he was in fact a revolutionary; others, a pacifist, because he preached love of enemies and forgiveness, but his revolution was an interior revolution and made harsh demands on his followers for a change of heart.

Easter removed him from both alternatives. He was neither a guerrilla nor a pacifist. The hope of his kingdom was elsewhere than in the political order. It was the kingdom of God, beginning now, fulfilled in eternity.

The hope of his kingdom, made possible on Easter, made him neither indifferent to the signs of the times nor impatient with them. The year of favor he announced would come in resurrection time, in Easter time.

The promise of the kingdom of God is not intended to loll us to sleep, or pacify us with futuristic dreams of a better world. The message of Jesus loses none of its reality on Easter Sunday. The promise of the kingdom is not to make us indifferent to the message. The promise of the kingdom is not an invitation to bring it about by force. It is God's kingdom we are building, not ours.

Jesus liberated us on Easter Sunday so that we could be free from sin, free from death, free from selfishness, free to begin building the kingdom on earth. That's the freedom, the liberation, that Easter brought to us.

The freedom as sons and daughters of God, new men and women, which Easter gives us, takes us right back to the message. It is our turn to bring glad tidings to the poor, to proclaim liberty to captives, recovery of sight to the blind, and release to prisoners.

Jesus was crucified and rose again to break the stranglehold of personified evil, so that this world might be fashioned anew, according to God's design, and reach its fulfillment.

The world is the theater in which grace and sin, both personal and social, are locked in a struggle: sin, in the form of egoism or selfishness and in the unjust structures of society; grace, in the form of selfless individuals and certain forms of community, cooperation, and association (Church, parish, family, for example). The world is the theater in which man and woman discover Christ.

We are an Easter people. Our year of favor from the Lord begins today.

Joyful People

WE are still in the afterglow of Easter, where the dominant theme is joy. We have been called an Easter people, a joyful people. But what is joy and how do we recognize it? Who is a joyful person?

I remember reading a few years ago about a prominent Protestant theologian and pastor who spent Easter at Mayo Brothers Clinic in Rochester, Minnesota. He had undergone some tests and was waiting in Rochester for the results. It was Easter Sunday, and he was separated from his wife and family as he feared the possibility that the tests might reveal a terminal disease. He was reflecting upon the meaning of death and resurrection.

He decided to spend Easter Sunday visiting various churches in the area — as a layman now, not as a pastor — and experience Easter from the pew. The experience was quite revealing. Instead of finding a joyful people celebrating the resurrection of Jesus, he found the Easter liturgies dull and unexciting. There was no real joy, not even in the homilies.

What is joy? How do we know when it is present and absent? It is a haunting question but has nothing to do with asking people to "Have a Happy Day." Is joy a peculiar Christian state of well-being? What are its roots? How does it differ from happiness, for example? The more I reflected upon the nature of Christian joy, the more I realized how difficult it is to describe it abstractly.

I began thinking back on some truly joyful people I have met, or some truly joyful occasions as a way to get a handle on Christian joy. The first person who came to my mind was an elderly woman, nearly ninety years old, who lived in a retirement home. The fact she was also my aunt and my godmother is beside the point.

Even though her mind is not quite as sharp as it once was, she is still one of those people who, at the age of ninety, lives almost in two worlds — very much like Our Lord after his resurrection. She is so close to Jesus in her constant prayers, the Mass, and the Eucharist, even in her dreams, that I have the feeling she somehow moves freely back and forth between heaven and earth, and in some ways has already had a foretaste of heaven. Some of her dreams reveal that.

But it is her positive attitude toward life and death and her intimacy with Jesus that make her a joyful person. Her constant joy, smile, hearty laugh, gratitude to God for all his blessings for her good life in a retirement home, for the nurses who attend her, the opportunity for daily Mass — these make her an Easter person. I cannot recall her complaining about anything, or saying an unkind word about anyone. She has won the hearts of the people around her. Martin Marty was right when he said you will find more genuine friendship in a home for senior citizens than in a singles bar.

What is the basis of her joy? It is her intimacy with the risen Lord. It is a deeply spiritual state and has nothing to do with material possessions, or the lack of them.

The occasion I call to mind as joyful, even though I did not experience it personally, was the meeting of Jesus with two of his disciples on the road to Emmaus, after his resurrection. What joy the disciples expressed later when they recalled the intimacy of the encounter, not knowing it was Jesus until they recognized him in the breaking of bread. "Did we not feel our hearts on fire as he talked with us on the road and explained the scriptures to us?" (Luke 24:32). Feeling our hearts on fire has to be at the very roots of Christian joy. The only comparable experience I can recall, and one that is familiar to priests everywhere, is the feeling of a "heart on fire" on my ordination day. I am sure young couples experience it on their wedding day as well. Or perhaps we have had the Emmaus experience when we are reunited with friends we haven't seen for a long time, or grandparents with their grandchildren, or the returning hostages with their families. At least there is human joy there.

Intimacy is the key word, and when it is intimacy with Jesus, or reunion with Jesus perhaps in the sacrament of Reconciliation, or in the Eucharist, Christian joy is the best way to describe the experience. It is something more than human joy.

The events that took place on the road to Emmaus were so commonplace to us all, they almost seemed uneventful. How often we have been down that road ourselves when we met someone along the way who gave us new life and set our hearts afire.

The two disciples were terribly distressed. It seemed as though the bottom had dropped out of their world. They were bereaved. Jesus had just been put to death. Their hopes were dashed. "We had hoped he was the one. . . ." Added to that, the rumor was that the tomb was empty and "they can't find Jesus." How abandoned and lost they felt when the stranger came along, listened to their tale of woe, then began explaining the Scriptures to them, why things happened as they did. "God's will."

Finally, as the day came to a close they recognized him in the breaking of bread and their hearts were inflamed with joy.

Laura, of Hamilton, Ohio, was such a person who brought joy to those around her, writes Louis. Laura died of cancer at age fifty-eight. She had been paralyzed from the waist down since age eighteen, and later became blind. "The Lord sent her my aunt," Louis writes, who herself was crippled with arthritis. For twenty years these two ladies were to share the same hospital room. Quick with her fingers, Laura was good at leathercraft and had her own little business.

When Louis's aunt eventually became blind, he visited the two ladies once, and the visit filled him with joy. Laura was reading to the aunt by fingering her Braille magazine. They are both dead now, but they brought much joy to those around them.

Eva White was another remarkable lady, Ellen Wilson writes. "She helped raise my father and two nephews. She was always there when we needed her. Her calm and firm belief that everything would turn out all right made us all optimistic. She taught me to read, write, ride a bike, and drive a car, and most important, to love one another and trust God." A remarkable lady from the neighborhood.

A lady from Kansas City sent me a joy-filled prayer written by her sister. The sister, who was suffering from depression and mental illness, is now back home with her family and working. Her healing came from a chain of prayers offered by friends and relatives. Once addicted to Valium, she now has inner peace.

Carol of Buffalo, New York, writes about her father and his deep reverence for family spirit and family traditions. "He inspired me to a true enjoyment of work and to appreciate Mom. Above all, by the way he prays and visits the elderly through the St. Vincent de Paul Society."

Domenica of Cleveland writes about her ninety-three-year-old mother, a poor immigrant widow and mother of five (two are dead). "Her physical handicap has not diminished her happiness and her friendship with Jesus. Weekly Communion, the rosary, and solitude in prayer late each evening" are her sources of joy.

I often wonder how Jesus felt along the road to Emmaus. We know how the two apostles were inflamed with joy once they recognized Jesus in the breaking of bread. Surely, it must have been an emotional moment for Jesus, too. Joy comes from giving as well from receiving.

Ann, from Evansville, expressed it well when she told how much joy she received cooking a Christmas dinner for a lonely and needy senior citizen. It brought joy to both of them.

Patrick, of Willows, California, writes a long story about his rebirth through the charismatic movement and how it involved his whole family. A long-suffering polio victim, he is doing for others now.

John, of Griffith, Indiana, found his joy in praying for those who injure us and in reconciliation.

Another lady from Britton, South Dakota, Mabel, has found joy in the charismatic movement. She has moved from "first effervescent joy" to a "firm life-giving flow of knowing, sometimes tinged with pain, as others share their heartaches with me in asking for prayers."

Mary, of Bellows Falls, Vermont, experienced her "heart on fire" twenty-two years ago, at age forty-five, on Good Friday. "I was reborn to a new life in Christ."

Giving birth to her first son and holding him the first time brought a moment of joy to Clare, of Minster, Ohio, who is now the mother of eight.

A mother from North Judson, Indiana, didn't hold her third child until this January, at age thirty-seven, born long after her other two, aged sixteen and nine. "I have found unexpected joy in this baby. It has brought my husband and me closer together."

And this touching letter from Marianne of Centerville, Virginia, tells what a joyful moment it was when she and her husband decided to have their third baby at home, with the help of a nurse-midwife. The baby was due around Christmas. Marianne writes, "After much prayer, we decided to make this baby an event to strengthen our family. Anticipating the birth of this baby made Christmas come alive for our children. As the time for delivery neared, friends and neighbors became involved."

Then the moment of joy. Marianne tells how, during the moment of his birth, Joseph was first touched by his dad, then held in the eager, joyful arms of his mother. "The feelings are almost impossible to describe — just a real closeness to Our Lord, our Creator. In just minutes, our children and friends were at our side gazing at and touching this beautiful boy."

Renewing her wedding vows on her twenty-fifth wedding anniversary, with their eight children present, brought a woman from Bloomfield Hills, Michigan, her greatest joy. The first six children were adopted, then God sent them two boys of their own conception.

Ruth of Wolcottville, Indiana, who has been in a wheelchair off and on, writes: "I found joy in the rising and setting sun, in the miracles of nature, especially in births of all kinds, in singing in tongues. Joy can stir the heart with fire until it almost could burst with pain.

The gift of the Miraculous Medal turned life around for one

lady, now forty, who has been promoting the wearing of the medal since. She was the victim of child abuse and led a life of sexual promiscuity until a friend gave her the medal. Her life changed dramatically.

Katherine, from Marion, Massachusetts, enclosed this beautiful statement of joy by Mother Teresa. I pass it along:

"Joy is prayer. Joy is strength. Joy is love. Joy is a net of love by which you can catch souls.

"God loves a cheerful giver. She gives most who gives with joy.

"The best way to show gratitude to God and other people is to accept everything with joy.

"A joyful heart is a normal result of a heart burning with love. Never let anything so fill you with sorrow as to make you forget the joy of Christ Risen."

In closing I want to share one other moment of personal joy with you, then I'll explain why it is so precious to me and why it arrived so unexpectedly. Some excerpts from a letter from my son Reese:

"Joy is having a friend to talk to in times of need.

"Joy is having enough money to buy food and gas.

"Joy is going to Mass on Sunday.

"Joy is flying to New York City in a 727.

"Joy is having a late night dinner there with a friend.

"Joy is experiencing loneliness and not going into a state of depression.

"Joy is walking down 42nd Street in New York city at 1:00 in the morning.

"Joy is work, play, and life.

"Joy is sitting here at 2:00 A.M. thinking about a friend who has been like a father I never had.

"Joy is looking at life in a positive way."

— Reese, Chicago, Illinois

What makes this so personally touching is that Reese is a young man I literally raised in Chicago. He has been like a son to me the past twenty-five years. I first met him in grammar school while I was a parish priest on the west side of Chicago. Recently, Reese and I had a beautiful weekend in New York City, and his joyful note alludes to that.

His thoughtful note brought unashamed joy to me, and what an unexpected gift from God it was. God's gifts bring joy.

Reese and I have been down the Emmaus road many times.

Might I suggest you and your loved ones — husband, wife, friends, family — take an Emmaus walk together this spring and feel the presence of Jesus.

We and the Holy Spirit

AFTER a battery of tests recently, I found out one of my physical problems is shortness of breath. Since I was a little boy, I recall problems with my breathing, and I recall my mother doctoring me for it most of my childhood. I attributed most of it to the damp Midwest, where everyone has a touch of sinus trouble, as we called it in Indiana.

I got to thinking about the importance of "breath" to life. When we can no longer breathe, we are declared dead. That's why the environmentalists are concerned about polluted air. We simply can't exist without air. Air, breath, pneuma, wind also, of course, have been associated with the Holy Spirit, ever since the Spirit of God hovered over the universe.

The power of breath, of wind, of air, that intangible we can't catch hold of, barely control or contain, blows as it wills and when it wills. How much we experience this during these blustery spring months, especially these forty days after Easter and before Pentecost.

Nature seems to reinforce our anticipation of the Spirit these balmy spring days. The soothing winds of spring can also turn into the cruel winds of tornadoes this time of year. Because of its unpredictability, the wind can blow when and how it wills. It can range from a whisper on a mountaintop, where the prophet Elijah heard it as the voice of God, to a destructive force that can destroy whole towns and homes, wreaking death in less than a second.

The Breath of God

So it is fitting that air, wind, breath whispers be identified through biblical history as the Spirit of God and as the Holy Spirit.

From the very first lines of Genesis through the Acts of the Apostles, the Spirit of God is a moving force. We read in Genesis that "in the beginning when God created the universe, the earth was formless and desolate. The raging ocean was engulfed in total darkness, and the power of God was moving over the water."

The Spirit of God was brooding over the dark vapors. And God spoke. The Word of God was the breath of God taking shape and creating the universe, dividing light from darkness, forming sky and oceans, earth and seas, plants and fruits, days and nights, sun and moon, the land with animals and reptiles. And the breath of God gave names to everything in the universe.

In the Old Testament, and even yet today, there is a difference between the breath of the nostrils and the breath of the mouth. The breath of God's nostrils symbolized his wrath, which descends as a storm on his enemies, whereas the breath of the mouth is life-giving. The breath of the mouth of God produced the life of man, when he created the first man.

It is same with us. When we are angry, we breathe through our nostrils. We snort. When we are loving and caring, we whisper, or we kiss. Our emotions are often very evident through our breathing, whether it be heavy, rapid, or palpitating.

In the Hebrew conception of nature, the wind is characterized by subtlety, rapidity, power, and docility, which are opposed to the terrestrial elements of earth, water, and inert masses.

Likewise in human beings, the elusive breath, fragile and vacillating, still in all can elevate the body and give it life, whereas the flesh is destined for the corruption of the grave. The Hebrews called this the Breath of God, the *ruah* of Yahweh. And Jesus will say later on: "It is the spirit that gives life; the flesh profits nothing." And St. Paul will speak of the letter that kills and the spirit that gives life.

All this means that we who are baptized in the Spirit must let ourselves be carried by the breath of God, alone capable of giving access to the intimacy of God. The place where the Christian adores in spirit and truth is the only place where the Spirit breathes: The Church of Jesus Christ.

For St. Luke, in the Acts of the Apostles, which deals in the beginning of the Church from that first Pentecost, the Holy Spirit is the great artisan of the infant Church. The Holy Spirit can still act as an all-powerful wind, but even when the wind is lacking, it is the impulses of the Holy Spirit that determine the ministry of the apostles. It is the Spirit who sends Paul and Barnabas to Seleucia from Cyprus, who forbids entrance to Asia. Throughout the Acts of the Apostles the Pentecostal winds never stop blowing.

Father Jacques Guillet, in *Themes of the Bible*, says, "the Spirit is the most mysterious of realities. He is everywhere in the Church. He is the source of the humblest of Christian actions as of the most exalted; he lives in the heart of every Christian, carrying on with the spirit of each one the dialogue which makes it live before God. How could he not be a person?

"Paul adores him, alongside the Father and the Son, and the Church baptizes in the name of three persons. Yet he has no proper face, no apparent personal function which sets its mark on him."

The Spirit of Jesus

UNLIKE the Word, who has his own physiognomy, and unlike the Father, who is visible in the Son, the Spirit has no such traits. He is as intangible as the wind. The Holy Spirit is the Spirit of Jesus, and that is the secret of his being. The New Testament reveals it to us.

The Spirit speaks of Jesus and moves toward the Father. "This is the secret which he whispers" in quiet confidences. The Holy Spirit infiltrates hearts in order to transform them, to open them to the Word, to make them his bearers and his martyrs.

That same Word of God, breathed by God, was in due time to become flesh in the form of God's only Son, Jesus Christ. That same Spirit of God was to come upon Jesus at his Baptism by John on the banks of the Jordan and at the time of the Transfiguration. It was the Spirit that Jesus himself would send upon his apostles and his Church at the time of the first Pentecost.

And it is the same Holy Spirit that was so familiar a companion to the early Church, as recorded in the Acts of the Apostles, that the account itself has been referred to by many as the Acts of the Holy Spirit. The apostles did nothing without the Spirit, so much so that the familiar words rolled off their tongues: "We and the Holy Spirit" did this, decided that, went here, evangelized there.

We are still bathing in the rays of the new hope brought about by the resurrection of Jesus. Hope has always been associated with the Holy Spirit.

When Vatican Council II was announced by Pope John XXIII, the good Pope suggested we read the Acts of the Apostles and relive the time when the disciples were together in the upper room preparing to receive the Spirit. Pope John prayed that the Lord "renew your wonders in this our day. Give us a new Pentecost."

With the coming of the Holy Spirit upon the apostles on that first Pentecost, as recorded in the Acts of the Apostles, the unfolding of the Holy Trinity — the Father, the Son, and the Holy Spirit — is complete. It will be up to the theologians later on to sort out the theological fine points of the doctrine of the Trinity — three divine persons, one God.

But for now the Scriptures have laid it bare. We have met God the Father-Creator of the Old Testament, the Word made flesh of the Gospels, and the ineffable works of the Spirit in the Acts of the Apostles.

As we celebrate Pentecost Sunday, we can now talk about relationships. It is the dynamic relationship of love between the Father, Son, and Spirit that gives us our model.

John's beautiful meditation in the Fourth Gospel on the relationship between the Father and the Son translates into the intense activity of the Spirit sent to us by the Father and the Son on Pentecost. It is an intense activity of love.

Human relationships are indeed love relationships, whether between lovers, spouses, friends, or family members. In each instance the feelings in different degrees are aspects of love. What the Trinity — three persons in one God — teaches is that the relationships depend first of all upon communication. The persons of the Trinity are in total communication with each other. There are no secrets among them, no surprises. The Father sends the Son, the Son loves the Father, the Holy Spirit proceeds from the Father and the Son.

Secondly, relationships are expressions of love — self-sacrifice, suffering, ability to give and receive love. When that kind of relationship is absent from our lives, we are lonely. Loneliness, not to be confused with aloneness or solitude, is the absence of love, the absence of a loving relationship with another. Nothing can be more destructive of the human psyche. It paralyzes and renders one helpless. Health and happiness depend on the ability to love and be loved, to feel worthwhile to ourselves and to others.

Again, back to the Triune God. The Father so loved the world that he gave us his Son. The Son so loved the Father that he fulfilled the Father's will until death on the cross. The Father and the Son so loved us they sent the Spirit to become the dynamic of their love in our lives.

If we love God, we will never be lonely, but we achieve that love of God not abstractly but when we are in relationship with others. The Father did not love us abstractly, but sent his Son Jesus. Jesus didn't love the Father abstractly, but fulfilled the Father's will by suffering and dying for us. The Holy Spirit is not some abstract and faceless force in the Church, but the Spirit of Jesus working through concrete human relationships.

Loneliness will always be a part of the human condition. Our hearts will always be restless until they rest in God. But with healthy, loving, intimate human relationships, we ought never to be isolated or separated from others. It is at this point that mental, physical, and spiritual health converge.

Pentecost Sunday is a good day to examine our relationships. Are we communicating? Is there love, self-sacrifice, suffering in our closest relationships? Remember that the apostles never said, "I and the Holy Spirit" but "we and the Holy Spirit." Our most intimate relationships must be "we" relationships.

Sacramentalizing Chicago

SOME dioceses around the country have been conducting Mercy days, or "Welcome back into the Church" days, with a great deal of success. They are often conducted during Lent, when priests are on call day and night in the rectory for people who want to come home, or reconcile with the Church, or simply to talk to a priest. There are no pressures, no hard sell, but simply an open invitation.

Well, I have yet another idea for evangelization. It came to me in Chicago, the week after Easter, when I visited, filled with the Holy Spirit and fresh with the early enthusiasm of the early Church after the first Pentecost. The Easter season is that time when all Christians ought to be on fire with the Spirit, after the glorious resurrection of the Lord.

The disciples in the early Church were sent forth to proclaim the Good News of salvation, the death and resurrection of Jesus. On Mercy days we invite the people to come to us, but there is a difference between going forth and inviting others to come to us. It is the difference between Jesus and John the Baptist.

This is where my new idea comes through, and I hope you won't be scandalized by it. I would like to see one day a year set aside when all priests, religious, deacons, and ministers of all denominations go forth from their churches and rectories and convents and homes into the bars and taverns in their communities to evangelize.

Let me share an experience from Chicago. I had made an appointment to meet a dear friend for dinner, a former secretary of mine when I was working in Chicago. When I arrived at the restaurant, she was waiting for me in the bar. Within minutes I met three of her friends — two truck drivers and a Honduran refugee. The lady bartender was also her friend. I felt like Jesus at the home of Levi.

The male friends welcomed me and said they had heard all about me. They were excited to meet a priest, and the conversation that followed proved their sincerity. They each had problems and wanted to talk. When I gave them my business card, so we could keep in touch, they treated the card as a sacramental, a holy card, almost like a relic. They said the cards would be held in reverence and placed among their prized possessions.

For them the card became a link with the Church, with a priest, and with Jesus. I was overwhelmed with their grasping for something to hold onto with their lives. The small cards became sacramentals for them.

A lovely young bartender put a small birthday candle in front of me on the bar, the kind restaurants use when serving a birthday cake. "Father," she said, "before you leave bless this for me. I need a change in my life." Bless it I did.

I held the small candle in her hand and mine. I told her it was her Paschal Candle, her Easter candle, and that the graces of Our Lord's resurrection would come upon her. The candle would symbolize new hope and new life for her.

Later, she joined us at our table and poured out her heart. She had been living in adultery with a married man and wanted help. I counseled her and promised God would bless her with a new life if she had the courage to break the relationship. She promised. The Easter candle had brought her hope.

All this happened April 3 in Chicago, the twenty-first anniversary of my ordination to the priesthood. What a way to celebrate! Lord, have mercy!

POSTSCRIPT:
Meet Me in Galilee: October 1993

In October 1993, I begin my official "retirement" from the Archdiocese of Chicago. I have moved out of Chicago to Lake Papakeechie in Indiana, where I have rented a small cottage as my retirement home. It is in the Fort Wayne-South Bend Diocese, about halfway between Fort Wayne and South Bend.

But I have no intention of "retiring" there. You see, during the week I have been invited by St. Joseph's College, Rensselaer, Indiana, to develop a Center for Newman Studies at the college and to move my office of the Venerable John Henry Newman Association from Chicago to St. Joseph's College.

I am excited about the prospect of developing a national Newman Center, not only for Newman studies but also for the Canonization Cause of Cardinal Newman. As for the center itself, we are naming it the Leo A. Pursley Center for Newman Studies, after the retired Bishop of Fort Wayne-South Bend, now ninety-one years old, for he has been a supporter of Newman's Canonization Cause since it was first begun in 1958. In his own right, Bishop Pursley is also a Newman scholar, and he has a warm regard for St. Joseph's College, having attended the academy at the college when he was just a thirteen-year-old boy.

As for me personally, I graduated from St. Joseph's in 1945 and am thrilled to go back to the beloved campus at age seventy to make a contribution to the college that first gave me a taste for Newman. I feel like a college freshman all over again, and the Precious Blood Fathers have welcomed me back into their community. Many of them I have known down through the years; some of them are former professors of mine who have had a tremendous influence on my life.

I look upon this as a four-year commitment to get the center started. Not only do we envision having an impact on the thousand-student college, as we try to integrate Newman studies in the already recognized Core Program of Liberal Studies, but also eventually to develop a center where Newman scholars from the United States and Canada can come for dialogue and research. We hope eventually to offer summer courses in Newman, sponsor a quarterly review of Newman studies, and offer Newman conferences. We have a wonderful board of advisors to direct the center, drawn both from within the college and outside of it.

The commitment of the college to Cardinal Newman is gratifying, and an expression of a long tradition of Newman interest dating back to Father Raphael Gross, C.PP.S., former president of the college, and continued by the current president, Dr. Albert J. Shannon, the first lay president of the college, who has worked unceasingly to make the center a reality. We began work on it last January, and now the center will have opened in October 1993. Above all, the center will give stability to the Newman Association, for which I am forever grateful.

"Lead Thou Me On," as I prepare for a new venture of faith, to use Newman's expression. On weekends I will be back at Lake Papakeechie to reflect and write about it.

Meet me in Galilee.

Affectionately yours, Father Vincent J. Giese.

Enriching new booklets
that fill your spiritual needs

Sharing Your Faith:
A User's Guide to Evangelization
By Bert Ghezzi
No. 169, $1.50.

What We Believe About the Saints
By J. Michael Miller, C.S.B.
No. 170, $1.50.

Forgiveness
By Archbishop Daniel E. Pilarczyk
No. 171, $1.50.

Mary in the Bible: Questions and Answers
By Rev. John H. Hampsch, C.M.F.
No. 174, $1.50.

Father Roberts' Guide to Personal Prayer
By Father Kenneth Roberts
No. 176, $1.50.

A Catholic Understanding of the Gospels
By Peter M.J. Stravinskas
No. 175, $1.50.